THE WORLD AS A NEURAL NETWORK

THE STORY OF AI AND OUR FUTURE

NIRAJA BANDI
ARGHYA CHAKRABORTY

INDIA · SINGAPORE · MALAYSIA

Notion Press Media Pvt Ltd

No. 50, Chettiyar Agaram Main Road,
Vanagaram, Chennai, Tamil Nadu – 600 095

First Published by Notion Press 2021
Copyright © Niraja Bandi & Arghya Chakraborty 2021
All Rights Reserved.

ISBN
Hardcase 978-1-63904-524-2
Paperback 978-1-63850-552-5

DEDICATION

This book is dedicated to entrepreneurs and innovators who have helped technology advance beyond the wildest imagination. We also dedicate this book to fighters for social justice and equality, who have helped the benefits of technological development, reach millions in all corners of the world.

CONTENTS

AUTHOR'S NOTE

We live in the so-called 'Information Age' where data is increasingly referred to as 'digital gold'. The data from our digital existence is processed by AI and guided by its recommender algorithms. Yet we understand very little of how social forces interact with the advances in technology. Here we explore complex topics like Race, International Politics, Government Surveillance, and Industry from the perspective of a society that is increasingly reliant on AI.

What will be the future of humanity with the growing role of Artificial Intelligence (AI)? Will our lives take a turn for the better or the worse? Will it usher in a new age of prosperity or result in the ruin of humanity? "The World as a Neural Network" deals with these questions through an analysis of our current interaction with AI.

In a series of essays on a wide range of subjects, bound together through the common thread of the growing impact of artificial intelligence on our society, the book encourages readers to explore the impact of artificial intelligence on their lives and in turn, how they can change the course of AI.

ACKNOWLEDGMENTS

We thank the authors Som Bathla and Sweta Samota, who have mentored us and helped us in our journey as writers and continue to inspire many like us. They helped us navigate the labyrinth of the world of publication.

Our colleagues deserve a special mention for their consistent support both professionally and personally. We appreciate their faith in us as well as the patience they have displayed.

Most importantly we thank our readers for having invested their faith and time in our work. We hope that we have been able to meet their expectations and this would be the beginning of a long association. The credit for the success of this endeavour lies with all of them.

FOREWORD

The world today wakes up to new realities every morning. The remnants of the nightmares associated with the panic inducing sights of blood dripped barbed wire fencing and the mushrooming dark clouds have long ago been relegated to the ignoramus alcoves of memory. The realities that prevail today on the other hand are more hallucinating, steeped in controversial implications and at times even grotesque.

Humans had evolved from cave dwellers and hunter–gatherers to a more respectable agrarian community over the ages where survival was paramount against several other species jostling for supremacy. Slowly, as evolution shoved humans from their primitive Diaspora to the higher echelons of metamorphosis, science started unravelling new insights to their basic theme of existence. Science prompted them to do away with several Gods that humans had previously associated to the various natural phenomena like rain, thunder, earthquake etc.

Today, humans have far outgrown the other more dependent and unintelligent species through its evolution into a supreme being. Humans have re-written the rules of survival. This transcendental descendant of the apes has managed to change the ecosystem in radical and unprecedented ways within almost 70,000 years of its existence. The new age developments in science and technology are already at par with that of the ice ages and the tectonic movements of pre-history. Within a century, that impact may surpass that of the asteroid that killed off the dinosaurs almost 65 million years ago.

Though, an asteroid had changed the trajectory of terrestrial evolution but could not alter the fundamental rules, which have remained fixed since the appearance of the first organisms about 4 billion years ago. During all those eons, whether it was an algae or a dinosaur, everything evolved according to the unchanging principles of natural selection. In addition, no matter what bizarre shape and form life may have adopted, it remained confined to the organic realm-whether a blade of grass or a hippopotamus, all were made of organic compounds. Now humankind is poised to replace natural selection with intelligent design and to extend life from the organic composition to the inorganic manifestations.

Charles Darwin, after a detailed study of several species at the legendary Galapagos Islands, had depicted the evolution of creatures through a graph within the axes of development and time. The graph of *Homo sapiens* or humans showed a steep incline to end up in a plateau up to the twenty first century. However, he had also created a miniature graph depicting the rise of an unknown species at double the speed. That race was predicted to overtake the human hegemony by 2050. After chasing several hypotheses in search of a conclusive inference, we have come to identify AI (Artificial Intelligence) to be the next dictator of civilization.

In the year 1818, Mary Shelley with the able aid of her husband Percy and the ever-benevolent Lord Byron had penned down the historic tale of *Frankenstein.* Though, it represented the science fiction genre for long, it has started looking closer to reality now. Not necessarily will AI develop into another fiendish humanoid, however, the fear for uncertainty always lurks amongst the shadows of speculation.

Niraja Bandi and Arghya Chakraborty, two gifted writers-researchers have researched through time to conjure up a manuscript that tries to decipher the age that humans are entering into. The in-depth analysis of the revolutionary phase heralded in by the evolution of AI is educative as well as cautionary. Though, we are still confronted with the dilemma about the degree of convenience or inconvenience this revolution in technology will cause to the generations ahead, we must admit that AI has penetrated and impacted several lives already. Are we just exercising our finesse to ideate or are we on a tryst to emulate God?

This book is a voyage towards a distant destination. I implore the naïve, the creative, the impressionable, the cynic, the genius, the stoic and all other forms of humans to embark on this journey through the rich pages of information. Whether you like it or not, change is imminent and therefore it is advisable either to be part of the change or be educated about the change.

Satadal Lahiri

Author, Consultant, Engineer, Exponent of TOC (Eliyahu Goldratt Foundation)

"There is more treasure in books than in all the pirate's loot on Treasure Island."

– Walt Disney

"No entertainment is so cheap as reading, nor any pleasure so lasting."

– Mary Wortley Montagu

In every sentence of a book beats the heart of its author. Each seed gives a sacrifice, that the sapling be born. A book too is a teacher. Books are immortal and become fossils of intellectual treasures in time. If the words and emotions in a book do not create an explicit scandal in the heart of its readers, the book is useless. I have known Niraja Bandi, as an amazing and intense author. She is also a great human being. Niraja has a literary heart and her books are on Women Empowerment and this masterpiece on an intriguing topic of 'Artificial intelligence' invokes a mental stupor. I think, one can never thank the author, enough for a book. This book is a treat for the ink drinkers, All the blitzkrieg of the new age makes no dent to natures poise. Nature is never in a hurry but always on time. I do not know much about artificial intelligence, but suspect it will expose my digital illiteracy. The best inventions are those that make the world more human and a better planet.

I Wish her Mind-Blowing Success.

Dr. Kamal Murdia,

MBBS, MS, MCh (Plastic Surgery), CS(UK)
Plastic -Cosmetic Surgeon - Author
Celebrated International Speaker
Mumbai, Maharashtra, India
Author: International Best seller- The
Million Dollar Powerful Personality.
The Strange case of the Billion Dollar Tortoise
www.drkamalmurdia.com

PREFACE

The book is the culmination of the authors' own initiatives to understand the growing integration of Artificial Intelligence (AI) with our daily lives. Most students in this country have very little idea about how AI is transforming the job market, as do most professionals, who are in various fields that are currently being transformed in the hands of AI. We continue to have passive interaction with increasingly complex AI technologies in our day-to-day lives without realizing what impact it currently has on our society and more importantly, the common future of humanity. This project is our attempt to make sense of the changes that are being driven by AI and our attempts to adjust to these.

Our greatest challenge isn't to grasp the technological aspects of AI but rather its social dimensions. While lines of code can be debugged, transforming society isn't simply a matter of changing a few laws. One thing that we have come to realize is that the major problem with our contemporary approach to AI is our inability to engage across disciplinary boundaries beyond a certain extent. Most of the brilliant minds of our times thus continue to work without being able to appreciate what happens beyond the boundaries of their domain. This approach is a direct impediment to our own appreciation of the advances made in the field of AI as cross-domain interaction has been one of the best ways to advance AI.

However, engaging across domains is challenging. Given the extended period of isolation in which different academic and corporate departments have remained, integrating these disparate interests can be a major challenge. Anyone who has worked in the industry will find a degree of antagonism exists between Human Resources, Marketing, Finance and other departments. This is a truism that holds pretty much across all sectors. Yet AI is rendering these boundaries redundant in many cases and forcing them through interaction, an experience both authors can personally attest to. This is one of the major reasons that we have embarked on this endeavour.

Our insights here are by no means unique if individual snippets are taken. The research that we have cited is already largely in the public domain, albeit in a scattered and unorganized manner. While the technologies of AI are driven largely in the domain of data science, inputs from social scientists and from the humanities may prove to be crucial in the domain. This might however prove to be extremely difficult given our increasing reliance on technocratic expertise in nearly all fields.

This overreliance is a recipe for unmitigated disaster as the University of Illinois, Urbana-Champaign, discovered the hard way. A pair of physicists Nigel Goldenfeld and Sergei Maslov had developed a model that they confidently proclaimed would allow the university to open up for students to attend physical classes. It relied on regular testing, contact tracing, as well as analyzing the behaviour of students in their interaction. The model was extremely detailed, even taking into account the spread of aerosol particles that might account for the spread of the virus. Yet the virus spread among the students with greater rapidity than even the most pessimistic estimates of the physicists presented. What went wrong? Apparently, the physicists hadn't taken into account the fact that students would not take the guidelines seriously and would attend parties even as they were tested positive and advised to quarantine. It would be improper to blame Goldenfeld and Maslov, given that they were far beyond their domain of expertise and operating in territory that was uncharted even for epidemiologists. It would be 'common sense' for many of us to assume that students, meeting their friends for the first time in months, would be unable to resist the temptation of flouting COVID-19 safety guidelines. But modelling the intricacies of human behaviour isn't as easy a task as many purport it to be.

We ourselves have come to recognize and appreciate the necessity of incorporating interdisciplinarity in our previous work *Empower to Transform*, where we explored the various facets of women's empowerment, which has further encouraged us to engage in the various facets of interdisciplinary research. This, of course, reflects a broader trend within academia, where interdisciplinary and comparative research has increasingly found relevance and foothold with many departments specifically emerging in order to integrate researchers working in diverse fields.

One specific example would be the growth of critical race theory, which has kicked up a huge storm in US politics. While traditional anthropology and sociology to a great extent have confined and contented themselves with studying the behaviour of different social groups, critical race theory has gone beyond the traditional domain of these fields and has managed to become an integral part of sensitizing various government departments and even private firms on the impact of race in decision-making. This has recognizably made certain people quite uncomfortable as they are forced to grapple with the implications of the fact that they have benefitted from racialized hierarchies in the United States. Critical race theory relies on the insights provided by Critical Theory, which emerged in the inter-war period in Frankfurt, Germany, and has repeatedly emphasized the interaction between the disciplinary domains of sociology, economics, political theory, psychology and others. Formulations of various critical theorists like Theodor Adorno and Max Horkheimer have played an invaluable role in our own recognition of the role of AI in modern life, which we hope that our readers will take cognizance of and proceed further.

Our own enquiry of the role played by AI in facilitating oppressive and racist structures is at least in part inspired by works like *Algorithms of Oppression* by Safia Noble. This necessitates us to grapple with the quite uncomfortable fact that society as we understand it provides us with very little freedom if any at all. Most of us are likely to live and die within the same conditions, and we work not as 'free' individuals providing labour in exchange for payment, but by necessity. Our skills are socially determined rather than acquired through hard work, as purported by our contemporary economic myths. These economic realities manifest in many forms of social hierarchies all around the world like caste in South Asia and race in the Western world. Isabel Wilkerson in *Caste: The Origins of Our Discontents* perform a cross-sectional analysis of these very structures, pointing out how they operate in similar manner despite the widely varying circumstances of the United States and South Asia. We have pointed out that when AI algorithms seemingly violate the presumed 'neutrality' of these structures, what it often exposes is the very foundation of the myth of equality and opportunity.

Another key theme that we have sought to analyse here is the basis of electoral democracy and the mythical entity of the 'informed voter'. Information, at least real information, is a function of privilege in our world. This we can see in the world of finance where people, who can pay to access financial advisors, are the ones least likely to lose money in the stock market or other forms of investment. With the growth of political consultancies and the precision that AI-based algorithms offer them to target voters with both information and misinformation, it has become a major concern for the future of electoral democracy as we understand it. On the other hand, it also exposes a fundamental flaw in the once unassailable concept of electoral democracy, which had remained only a theoretical concern for a long time. The problem of the real voter is that he is only partially informed or uninformed on the vast majority of the issues that are at play during an election. Simply banning misinformation will only create another issue of censorship that will further undermine trust in the political system. One issue is that we have a single vote that we can cast every few years. Major political systems thus tend to condense around a select few political positions that are shuffled around every few elections. The unviability of third parties in the US is a major demonstration of the fact, which is despite the reality that their positions do reflect the actual political stance of the vast majority of Americans. Rather than fostering a culture of debate and discussion, as should happen in a healthy democracy, what we tend to see is the proliferation of a 'culture war', where the populace is divided along the political battle lines. This is another uncomfortable question that begets no easy answers, especially for those who have been brought up believing in the natural superiority of electoral democracy to other possible alternatives.

AI also challenges our traditional conception of labour and labour-relations. The basic assumption, perhaps since the beginning of our economic system had been that we provide labour in exchange for other things that provide sustenance. This reflects the simple idea of a barter-based economy that had been in function at the dawn of human civilization. However, in the modern capitalist system, production isn't simply for the purpose of sustenance but rather for a global surplus of commodities. This surplus production goes above and beyond what we collectively need for our basic sustenance and is deliberately designed to be in excess of what is required. This allows different firms to compete on the market by offering lower prices than their competitors. Here, however, two major problems emerge within the domain of the global capitalist system. The first is the problem of the 'anarchy of production', since we have very little idea going into the process of production about how much of the outcome is viable in the market, this generates an enormous amount of economic uncertainty, both for the corporates and more importantly, for its employees. Since most producers are uncertain of how much of the same commodity is being produced by other producers, there is an incentive for overproduction, leading to price uncertainties in the market. These uncertainties in the market, on the other hand, lead to the second problem that plagues capitalism and underconsumption. Consumers cannot rationally utilize their earnings as the market for both commodities and jobs remains uncertain, thus withholding a large part of their incomes as savings for possible future uncertainties. Uncertainties are also rendered by the possibility of unemployment as certain businesses are displaced largely due to the chaotic and unscientific mode of market competition. This means that the purchasing power of workers drops even further and there is a resultant economic crisis. These economic crises have been a regular phenomenon of our capitalist structures and have been a major point of enquiry for a large number of economists.

AI transforms this market in two distinct ways. First, it poses the ability to do away with market uncertainties on the consumer end. The rise of AI-based algorithmic data-mining has allowed companies to study clients and consumer behaviour well beyond what was possible in pre-AI days. On the other hand, AI ramps up the productive capabilities of simple human labour cutting down on the cost of training as well as speeding up production time. While it is a good thing in general, the problem lies with the fact that these may lead to unemployment for a large number of workers, which in turn has ripple effects on consumption. This is something that we have specifically paid attention to in the book. Multiple solutions to the problems are imminent as AI gains deeper penetration into the economy, with the proposals for a Universal Basic Income being one of the most widely known. Yet it isn't clear if the vast majority of the public will support the idea that certain people will be given money to do nothing, even if it is known to result in positive growth in the economy. Thus, we have emphasized not simply on policy change but rather engagement and dialogue that can result in greater understanding in the manner in which the economy is changing, but also how it will benefit all sections of the economy.

Different countries are forced to reckon and grapple with the fact that these transformations are taking place, and these have resulted in wildly distinct outcomes. In this book, we have discussed the roles played by the Chinese government and the governments within the European Union. Essentially, the standard response has been to ensure that the government retains a framework through which they can determine if any company can access the user data of their citizens. Of course, the Chinese government's response goes far beyond these simple regulations and has led to it becoming the sole arbiter of the data of Chinese users on the internet. The Chinese government already has an enormous role in domestic production, and by being able to control the consumption patterns of the Chinese people, they have a grip on both aspects of the economy. We have also demonstrated that in the case of countries that do not have a stable economy or governments, AI though useful, can bring many pitfalls in its wake, with the African region being its prime example.

This scuttling of traditional relations of production and consumption has led to certain sections of the economy being rendered unviable. One of the most visible impacts has been that on the mainstream media. With news being widely and freely available on Social Media, the viability of traditional media houses has come under question. Most media houses are being forced to rely on ad revenue rather than user subscriptions, which, in turn, mean that media houses are forced to create what is known as 'clickbait' news, a form of empty sensationalism. Certain governments like those in Australia have sought a remedy by making social media sites pay media houses, whose links are shared on their platforms. This, however, has not proven to be an easy path.

Most of us have approached AI through pre-existing notions precisely because we are still trying to understand when and how it will affect our lives. Many have filtered it through the framework of the industrial revolution when the process of industrialization destroyed livelihoods for millions in Europe, ushering in an era of extreme poverty while at the same time unleashing the scourge of colonialism all over the world. After all, we have seen the result of automation in the manufacturing sector in the United States and the devastation it has caused to communities that had relied on the manufacturing economy. A similar process has been replicated where lower wages have led to mass outsourcing of certain manufacturing jobs and even services, with Indian IT workers often derogatorily referred to as 'IT Coolies'. On the other hand, others have waxed eloquent about the utopian future that we will enjoy in an AI-led world. Such optimism, though inspiring, has no real basis in our existing reality. Our contemporary society doesn't allow for an equitable distribution of the benefits of technology. It would be the height of naivety, as we have highlighted time and again that problems in our contemporary society could be simply done away by particular technological achievements. This approach assumes that inequalities, fostered by racial, gender or other social biases, are simply a factor of time, which they aren't. Rather, they are recreated, as with issues like redlining and segregation, by the very social structures that benefit from these inequalities. Thus, a conscious effort must be made towards eradicating these inequalities if we are to actually imagine a utopia fostered by technological advancement.

Within the pages of this book, we have addressed a host of issues, including the ones that we have discussed above. We hope that the reader will find them nearly as enlightening as the authors have had in composing it.

01. INTRODUCTION: A BRAVE NEW DIGITAL WORLD

"The old world is dying, and the new world struggles to be born. Now is the time of monsters."

– Antonio Gramsci

The proliferation of Artificial Intelligence (AI) across multiple fields globally has had a transformational role in the way human societies interact and function. Fields like social media, healthcare, education, finance, agriculture, etc. are increasingly receptive to the implementation of AI. However, this doesn't mean that this implementation has been uniform or universal and has had various implications all over the world. Yet there is a glaring lack of understanding of the ways how AI is transforming the world in which we inhabit. People tend to think that AI is a distant dream, often influenced by its representation in popular culture, where very often we find sentient robots trying to dominate or eradicate humanity. This confrontationist attitude is the result of entrenched fears, as technology has usually been employed to the immediate detriment of workers in certain industries.

Let's make something clear. We are not arguing about some hypothetical apocalypse that will befall us if we do not stop the rise of the 'sentient robots'. Quite the contrary, we hope to establish that AI has the potential to bring a positive transformation, but only and only if we are willing to make the necessary changes to our own social structures. It is easy to make alarmist claims, especially given that we have failed to effectively integrate the relatively low level of AI that currently exists into our socio-economic structures. The multifarious results of such mal-integration have been explored in this book. As we have noted throughout the chapters, AI continues to very much replicate existing social and economic relations, often highlighting problems that pre-exist within our societies.

What is Artificial Intelligence?

Alan Turing, the mathematician and philosopher, who helped crack the Nazi 'Enigma Code', which was a major reason behind the defeat of the Germans in World War II, turned his mind towards the question of 'intelligence' of machines[1]. The fundamental question he asked was, can machines think? Computers have, in general, been used for the purpose of aiding human tasks for decades, but usually, these tasks were mainly confined to the processing of data rather than understanding the meaning of said data. Turing was asking if the role of human interpreters of data could altogether be eliminated by machines. Artificial Intelligence itself refers to a vast array of technologies that operate in very different areas;

---

1   https://www.csee.umbc.edu/courses/471/papers/turing.pdf

however, these technologies seek to answer Turing's question in the affirmative. One of the key features of AI is its ability to 'learn' from its interactions. This is achieved through Artificial Neural Networks (ANNs) that simulate the function of neurons in human brains, which are trained in order to recognize patterns in data and react accordingly. Programs that allow ANNs to learn by accessing data themselves are a part of a process called Machine Learning.

If we are to break down the development of AI, we can identify three distinct periods of development. Between the 1950s and 1970s, marking the first phase of the development of AI, the basic ideas of neural networking were first formulated[2]. This was followed by the period between the 1980s and 2010s, when Machine Learning became popular, marking the second phase. The recent development in the field has been that of Deep Learning, where AI's learning abilities can scale with the availability of data marks the ongoing third phase. It is in this period that AI has become increasingly integrated with everyday life as the wide-spread use of the internet makes the processing of copious amounts of data necessary.

AI in Contemporary Times

Currently, AI has widespread applications in various fields including cybersecurity, logistics and supply chains, manufacturing, healthcare, and even in the improvement

---

2   https://www.sas.com/en_in/insights/analytics/what-is-artificial-intelligence.html

of workplace communication. Siri and Alexa have literally become household names and have become integral to the daily organization of many homes. In certain areas like flying and driving, AI plays the role of an assistant, helping pilots and drivers make crucial decisions, and it is predicted that AI will be equipped to take up a more proactive role soon. Another key area that uses AI-based recommender systems is that of social media sites like Facebook, Twitter, Instagram or YouTube. These sites use recommender algorithms in order to analyse the preferences of their users and provide content based on this analysis.

It has been pointed out that AI companies like BlueDot had alerted hospitals around the world of a bump in pneumonia cases in Wuhan, China on 30th December, nine days before WHO flagged COVID-19. This being said, it is unlikely, as *MIT Technology Review* points out, that solely relying on AI might not be the most sensible strategy[3]. It has been pointed out that several media outlets and Wuhan medical bulletins have also flagged the outbreak on the very same day. This demonstrates that AI is yet to surpass humans in terms of flagging disease outbreaks. This doesn't mean that AI cannot play any role in mitigating the crisis presented by the COVID-19 pandemic. One major area where AI is currently playing a major role is in the development of vaccines, with AI helping researchers understand the

3   https://www.technologyreview.com/2020/03/12/905352/ai-could-help-with-the-next-pandemicbut-not-with-this-one/

structure of the virus as well as shortlist potential vaccine candidates, cutting down time, which would otherwise have taken months. In fact, bioengineering is being used for the development of vaccines against other types of flu and even HIV, with copious amounts of help for AI. The time-consuming aspects of vaccination such as human trials cannot be eliminated by AI.

Another major area that has seen (and helped) the expansion of AI is that of social media, an aspect which has received attention in this book. Given the popularity of SM platforms, they have played a major role in expanding the availability of publicly available data of users on the internet, helping with the growth of the field of Deep Learning that requires precisely the availability of uncategorized data in order to be able to grow and expand. This, of course, has given us a major reason to be concerned, especially regarding the use of our private data to compile statistical models, which we shall have no meaningful control over.

The Discourse

The initial chapter of the book, titled *The Cambridge Analytica Kerfuffle*, looks into the controversy stoked by the exposure of the operations of Cambridge Analytica, a data analytics company, which used AI to study the behaviour of voters from the information available on social media platforms. Not only has this led to the question of the security of user data on major social media platforms like Facebook, but also the very sanctity of democracy in the age of AI. These questions overflow into the next chapter, titled *China's Social Credit Model*; it takes a look at the very undemocratic nature of the Chinese state's intrusion into the private domain. We have argued that while the Chinese state has effective means of controlling the behaviour of its citizens, what it seeks to control is the consumer behaviour of its citizens. We believe that together these two chapters will help readers understand how AI can go far beyond its initial scope of usage, even with the comparatively low level of technological progress that the field has seen.

The three chapters that follow, *Industry, Automation and the Rust Belt in the US*, *Artificial Intelligence and the Question of Racial Justice*, and *From Wall Street to Washington*, have a particular focus on the United States, which we believe that readers from other parts of the world shall find highly informative nonetheless. We believe that the focus on the United States is justified given the oversized impact its domestic politics has on international relations and trade due to its position as a global superpower. These chapters explore the relationship between the various social groups in the US and how AI mediates between these relationships. The first of these explores the changes that have occurred in the American industries, especially the decline of manufacturing and the impact this has had on towns, cities and, sometimes, entire states that relied on the manufacturing sector. The relationship between automation and the uneven development that it engenders is a major area of exploration in the course of this chapter. The second deals with the interaction between race and AI and how existing racial inequalities and discrimination find expression through artificial intelligence. We have demonstrated how existing social inequalities can and do find their way into models that help AI systems learn. Once these biases are factored into the AI, they can help perpetuate the problem, even in places where race isn't explicitly mentioned. The third explores the role of social media in the Left-Right binary that exists in the United States and how recommender algorithms have played a crucial part in the formation of this binary division. Here, we take a look at the origin of movements like Occupy Wall Street and how they presented a challenge to the establishment politics of the US, helping create a new political language, using social media as a key link in their mobilization, thus bypassing the need for the mainstream media. Soon enough, right-wing movements like that of QAnon took up similar routes in order to create an entire ecosystem based on conspiracies, which saw its ultimate expression in the riots on the US capitol on 6th January 2021.

The chapter titled, *Artificial Intelligence and Work Culture*, deals with the question of labour in the age of AI. Since the industrial revolution, humans have worked under the assumption that while work that requires physical labour is easily replaceable and bound to be overtaken by technology with time, the growth of

AI demonstrates that even work that requires 'human' intelligence is not safe from automation. While this has evoked a strong debate whether AI is going to take over our jobs, we argue that these changes should prompt us to think more in terms of consumption rather than production. The following chapter deals with *Artificial Intelligence in Africa* and looks at the historic transformation of the continent under circumstances of colonialism, which resulted from the industrial revolution in Europe. This brings us to the crucial question of how different the AI revolution will be in terms of its impact on the African people. Understandably, many are apprehensive, given that most of the AI companies are based in Europe and North America and can potentially result in a repeat of the colonial experience. We also explore a number of AI-based companies that have started operating in Africa and how they are transforming the lives of the people.

The final chapter, titled *The European Model for Data Privacy,* looks at the ongoing contradictions between data privacy and the data-driven AI technologies that characterize cyberspace in the European Union. This marks a growing challenge to the idea of a world integrated through improvements in technological developments, as the conceptualization of political sovereignty seems to be at loggerheads with such concepts. This also underlines once again that the growing challenges, that advance in the world of tech, can present to the established economic order worldwide.

The Reality of AI

In the 1980s and 1990s, a number of sci-fi films from Hollywood depicted a dystopian future that would result from AI. Popular franchises, like the *Terminator* and *Matrix* series, depicted a future where an apocalyptic clash between humans and robots was inevitable. These resulted from a primordial fear that had been implanted into our social psyche by the devastation of the industrial revolution. In the current day, the *Black Mirror* series deals with the questions posed by the advancement made by technology, but in a very different manner. No longer are we fearful of being supplanted by the sentient robots, but rather our apprehensions now emerge from our own societies interacting with AI in a particular manner. The changing view of AI demonstrates our own insecurities rather than any concrete theorization of the trajectories that AI research has taken.

That doesn't mean that we should be at liberty to brush away these questions as mere apprehensions. The fears reflect the very real processes that are taking place within our world. We have friends with whom our friendships have withered because they have become obsessed with some conspiracy theory they found on the internet. The sales of this book will be reliant on an algorithm, that will recommend the book to the users, which are beyond the means of control of the authors. Given the ubiquity of AI in crucial areas like healthcare and driving, it means that an algorithmic error may be the difference between life and death. Of course, one may stand to reason that human errors are more, rather than less likely, but such logic is small comfort given the loss of control that we may start to feel as more aspects of our lives are entrusted to AI.

What we hope to do through the course of this book is illuminate the reader the way in which AI is already an indispensable part of our lives. Each of the following chapters deals not only with the technological aspect of AI but also with their social dimensions, which are often overlooked in a technocratic discourse. AI fundamentally relies on human interaction to be able to function and defines its existence in relation to these interactions, and it is crucial for us to understand how these processes are to be navigated. This doesn't mean that we are advocating for training all students in advanced computing (though understanding how AI works is increasingly becoming a basic 'soft skill' and a case may be made for it to be a part of school curricula). What we hope readers will realize is that confronting our fears of a technological takeover requires us to understand what we are actually afraid of.

02. THE CAMBRIDGE ANALYTICA KERFUFFLE

"We feel free because we lack the very language to articulate our unfreedom."

– Slavoj Žižek

When the Facebook-Cambridge Analytica scandal broke, most of us knew little about what to make out of it beyond the attention-grabbing headlines[4]. Surely, advertising on Facebook wasn't a crime, and the use of metrics to sharpen the accuracy of one's outreach couldn't be categorized as a criminal activity by any stretch. Cambridge Analytica (CA) claimed that it has simply aggregated publicly available data on Facebook to create its data set. CA's work was found to be in violation of UK privacy laws, and even Facebook was fined for the violation of privacy that occurred under its watch. The effect of the transgressions that CA had committed was far more intangible but at the same time, a graver threat to the democratic foundations of our society[5].

---

4   The Netflix documentary film *The Great Hack* will give readers a detailed insight into the scandal.

5   A timeline of the Cambridge Analytica scandal can be seen here: https://www.cnbc.com/2018/04/10/facebook-cambridge-analytica-a-timeline-of-the-data-hijacking-scandal.html

How Cambridge Analytica Hacked Democracy

The CEO of CA, Alexander Nix, bragged that the company had 5,000 data points on every American voter, which was revealed in a *Channel 4* expose. Carole Cadwalladr, a journalist with *the Guardian*, exposed the role played by CA in a series of critical elections, including the 2016 US Presidential elections and the Brexit vote in the UK. It was revealed that an app developed by Aleksandr Kogan, a Moldovan-American data scientist, named 'This is your digital life', was used to collect the data of millions of Facebook users[6]. Data of up to 80 million users were harvested and used for several political campaigns in multiple countries, including the 2016 Republican primaries and the Brexit vote in the UK. The distinguishing feature of CA was the manner in which it created a psychological profile out of the database and utilized this knowledge to target the section it had designated as the most vulnerable to its propaganda. Julia Carrie Wong, a reporter with *The Guardian,* pointed out that rather than infiltration and subterfuge, what had really happened was that CA had used Facebook precisely as it was designed to[7]. The amassing, extraction and exploitation of data is a key feature of Facebook itself.

6   https://www.theguardian.com/uk-news/2018/mar/21/facebook-row-i-am-being-used-as-scapegoat-says-academic-aleksandr-kogan-cambridge-analytica

7   https://www.theguardian.com/technology/2019/mar/17/the-cambridge-analytica-scandal-changed-the-world-but-it-didnt-change-facebook

CA's database enabled it to target crucial voters in the 'swing states' in the US. Rather than appealing to the general-consensus of the voters and attempting to swing said-consensus in the direction of a particular candidate, CA used tactics that sought to fundamentally polarize the voters into mutually exclusive and opposing camps. The targeted advertisement was used in order to demonstrate how fundamentally opposed to each group the 'other' camp was. Not to say that before the emergence of targeted advertisement, all Americans were in a state of harmonious co-existence[8]. As a matter of fact, many have pointed out that CA's tactics were successful precisely because of deep structural divergences within American society. However, a cynical target to deliberately manipulate voters, rather than attempting to inform them in order to enable them to make a choice that affects the long-term health of our democratic institutions, seems to be shady at best.

The unstated crime that CA was guilty of is the 'hacking' of democracy itself. While being fair, all political campaigns in history have, to some extent, sought to manipulate the public will. What CA had done was to convert the 'art' of political rhetoric into a 'science' of nearly pure numbers. Politics is, thus, hollowed out of its ideological content and invested in the cold, hard digits. Humans with distinct interests are pigeonholed into select categories that override their own unique political identities. As we shall discuss in the following sections, this leads to a particularly toxic form of polarization that

---

8 https://www.orfonline.org/expert-speak/divided-america-world/

kills any opportunity for debate and discussion. It has, in fact, been pointed out that the techniques that CA has employed, had been honed and perfected in Iraq and Afghanistan by the US Army to subjugate the population in those countries and whittle down resistance to a foreign regime[9]. In essence, if not in substance, CA had waged a war against the people of the United States. Yet the question arises, to what extent does such targeting work? Are people really influenced to such a significant extent by political ads?

The Filter Bubble

In the text *The Filter Bubble: What the Internet is Hiding from You*, Eli Pariser explains how the internet and the algorithms powered by AI can essentially trap us in a 'filter bubble' where we are rarely exposed to contradictory views. One such example would be the development of Neo-Nazi digital forums and the development of online ecosystems devoted to such politics. The emergence of an earnest 'flat-earther' movement is an alternate expression of the same filter bubble phenomenon. We have experienced this phenomenon ourselves when recommender algorithms on platforms like YouTube seem to only recommend a particular category of video to us.

Since most social media platforms are reliant on ad revenue, they rely on AI-based recommender systems that aim to grab the attention of the user for the longest amount

9   https://www.opendemocracy.net/en/dark-money-investigations/
    cambridge-analytica-is-what-happens-when-you-privatise-military-
    propaganda/

of time. Thus, 'clickbait' and sensationalism become a dominant phenomenon on most social media sites, erasing any trace of a nuanced dialogue on digital forums. In fact, research demonstrates that consumption patterns online have a strong correlation with polarized networks that help diffuse conspiracy theories and rumours[10]. Most social media sites rely on efficient delivery of targeted ads for revenue and thus have precious little incentive except the occasional backlash to keep them on a straight path. Additionally, some researchers have pointed out that confirmation bias plays a major role in the creation of a filter bubble.

The commercialization of news media has resulted in most major news sites having a particular target demographic, usually based on their political preferences. As far as the emergence of newspapers is concerned, most news outlets have had a particular leaning. In fact, by the late 19th and early 20th centuries, news magnates wielded enormous political power and influence. However, with the emergence of social media, our own attention span has become a commodity. On the other hand, revenue models for news media have increasingly become dependent on ad revenue rather than subscriptions, as more and more people increasingly rely on online sources for the news[11].

---

10   https://doi.org/10.1073/pnas.1517441113

11   Studies by *Pew Research Centre* have demonstrated the increasing reliance of News media on advertising: https://www.journalism. org/2014/03/26/revenue-sources-a-heavy-dependence-on-advertising/

In order to understand the formation of 'filter bubbles', it is important to understand the revenue models of contemporary Social Networking Sites (SNSs) like Facebook, Instagram, Twitter or YouTube. We use these sites out of a natural impulse to socialize, which they fulfil for 'free'. However, the real service provided by these sites is not to its 'users' but to its 'clients', which are the advertisers, who pay for a slice of our attention. Since social media fulfils the role of social validation, it can have a degree of addictive effect[12]. At the same time, SNSs need to strike a balance between advertisement and user content, as too many ads tend to put users off the platform. This is the reason behind the development of 'Recommender Algorithms', which rely on AI, focuses on preserving the attention of the user for as long as possible. It does this through a process of trial and error, by which it develops a database of the interests of the user and his/her network on the platform. Very often, as SNS's are bought under a single conglomerate, these platforms are able to share their data across platforms. Essentially, if a user interacts with, likes, comments, and shares a particular kind of content, the more she is likely to find the same or similar content on her newsfeed. Thus, the AI is able to predict the usage patterns of the user and place ads strategically. The effect of such an algorithm is that the user is effectively enmeshed with content that he/she will rarely have any disagreements with. Eli Pariser,

---

12   https://www.bbc.com/future/article/20180118-how-much-is-too-much-time-on-social-media

as discussed above, points out that even search engines like Google, which we tend to believe to be unbiased, usually provide us curated search results depending on our previous search history and interests. Here, we realize that the 'filter bubble' is a phenomenon engrained within the way that the revenue model of SNSs is organized.

CA had effectively weaponized the 'filter bubble' to amplify the fault lines in US society, resulting in the fractious nature of politics in the US that we see today. In Europe, it sought to utilize anti-immigrant politics in order to channelize support for the campaigns it was involved with.

Social Media as a 'Spectacle'

Guy Debord, the French philosopher, had theorized the 'Spectacle' as an image of the real world, that is presented by the 'dominant mode of production' in order to justify its own presence. He argued that since humans are subjugated by the economy, they are automatically subjugated by the spectacle as well. Essentially, the spectacle is the conversion of real relationships between people into a relationship between images of the world mediated by its economic impulses.

While Debord was writing in the 1960s, what he had pointed out is perhaps even more relevant in hyper-consumerist society today. The spectacle is the abstract form of new media that helps us communicate with the world around us. Debord argues that since the media is dependent on revenue, the perspective of the world it shows will inevitably be influenced by the same interests. This led to media houses developing programming that allowed them to grab the largest possible number of eyeballs for the longest possible amount of time. This helped them pull the greatest share of ad revenue. This theory when applied to social media meant that SNSs would be increasingly interested in developing recommendation algorithms that were reliant on AI. Most SNSs eagerly categorize users based on their 'interests' that can be deduced from their online activity. While one represents only a fraction of the totality of one's views online, this eventually determines the content that the user would be exposed to.

What makes social media distinct from traditional media is the manner in which each user interacts with it in a completely different, if dynamic, manner. The results of a Google search will differ on the basis of one's previous history of interaction on the site. The recommendation algorithm on nearly every app relies on data from previous interactions either by the user or by users with similar interests. On the other hand, traditional media cannot differentiate the content that it provides its readers/viewers, at least not as dynamically as social media does today. This opens up the readership/viewership to the possibility of a wider pool of ideas they could interact with. Traditional media also is incentivized to interact with a wider range of viewpoints as it might help them gain new readership. Such incentives are largely absent for SNSs.

Debord points out that the politics that arise out of this are simply the poor imitations of real contradictions that exist. The task of politicians, rather than engaging in dialogue, becomes to pander to a polarized market demographic. This lies at the root of what has been dubbed as the 'Culture Wars'[13]. In such conditions, politicians aren't leaders of thought but leaders of the spectacle, actors who are moved and shaped by populist appeals rather than principled political stances. Trump exemplifies the convergence of all these extravagant trends, from playing an exaggerated version of himself to playing up stereotypes of immigrants as criminals. In fact, one of the reasons that Trump had managed to win in 2016 was that he had mastered the art of using the spectacle to his own benefit.

The role of CA in playing up the spectacle in a manner that favoured Trump cannot be understated. It has used its prolific mechanism for gathering data on US voters to rapidly inflame polarization, to an extent that has not been seen since the era of desegregation in the US. As discussed earlier, politicians targeted ads that highlighted to conservative voters how different liberals were from them and fundamentally incompatible their interests were. They highlighted liberal demands for inclusive bathrooms, gun control, LGBTQIA rights, and accessible healthcare, pointing out to conservatives that

---

13 Tom Nicholas on YouTube has an extremely engaging video on the culture wars, and I encourage all readers to go ahead and watch the video titled *A brief history of the culture wars* (https://youtu.be/ TJ8ws2dqqFg)

such reforms would be taken up, while problems that plague their own communities like the lowering standard of living and the neglect of the interior parts of the US with small communities, which bore the brunt of the recession in 2007-09. Social media allowed the divisions to be played up in a manner that had never been possible before. Trump's prolific habit of tweeting regularly helped him bypass whatever checks and balances could be posed to him while he was in office. He used social media in a manner that helped him pose as an 'outsider' to the establishment while having spent nearly his entire life being coddled in the arms of the establishment. Here lies the reality of the spectacle in the age of social media.

The Way Ahead

People, in general, have become increasingly aware of the ways in which social media can be used to manipulate political perspectives. The current drive by the US Federal Trade Commission to establish at least some degree of control over monopolies on social media is a welcome change. There needs to be some amount of democratic control over such powerful entities, and there needs to be a degree of accountability. Mark Zuckerberg has committed to introducing measures that bring greater transparency to the way advertising is done on Facebook. The 'DE platforming' of Donald Trump and other Right-Wing figures, from major social media platforms, after the riot on the Capitol, demonstrate that there exists a degree of susceptibility to public pressure on the part of SNSs. We as a society must learn to wield this power effectively and fairly.

One of the key measures that should be considered is to limit the use of user data for commercial purposes. The European Union has managed to enforce laws protecting the privacy of its citizens, which has served as a model for several countries. There needs to be a conscious uncoupling of the ubiquitous role of advertisement that has percolated into nearly all items of public consumption. We need to institute a global model where media houses and online news portals can subdue their reliance on ad revenue to keep afloat. It is also important to pressurize social media giants to reorient their recommendation algorithms towards functions that focus more on keeping users grounded in ongoing conversations rather than focusing on revenue maximization. It is up to us to start a conversation in this regard.

03. CHINA'S SOCIAL CREDIT MODEL

"What difference does it make to the dead, the orphans and the homeless, whether the mad destruction is wrought under the name of totalitarianism or in the holy name of liberty or democracy?"

– Mahatma Gandhi

In 2014, China announced a new social credit system; the implications of which shocked the world. The system could essentially rate the behaviour of a user and regulate his/her access to certain resources. Thus, for example, someone accused of financial malpractice could be barred from booking business flights or luxury hotels, without any recourse to a defined due process. While the Chinese government insists that the uses of the system will be benign, there remains the possibility that the system would be used to expand upon the surveillance state in China. The real question here is how did the Chinese state develop the ability to amass such large-scale surveillance data? Moreover, we must also seek to understand, based on precedents, the extent to which the Chinese state will go in order to maintain its grip on power. Given that China is emerging as a growing power in the world, these technological developments have immense implications for the future of democracy.

China's Historical Economic Transformation

In order to understand why the social credit model is being implemented in China, we must understand why the ruling Communist Party of China seeks to extend its control. More importantly, we need to understand why we have never seen mass-scale protests against the ruling party despite its great authoritarian tendencies. In fact, the legitimacy of the ruling party has seen increasing support from the people of China, who feel that the party has improved their conditions of living substantially[14]. Why then does the party need a surveillance mechanism that exposes it to accusations of infringement of democratic rights? What dynamic relations with the people does the party maintain at the grassroots level?

Modern China, much like most post-colonial nations, started out at the bottom, with famines, plagues and chronic problems. When the Communist party came to power in 1949 at the end of a brutal civil war, one of the first tasks it undertook was the destruction of the feudal economic structure of the country. Since landlords were extremely unpopular among the Chinese peasantry, the campaign became wildly popular and resulted in the peasantry spontaneously murdering landlords in many places. The land redistribution and collectivization set the stage for further reforms to the Chinese economy, which we shall take a look at soon (countries like India, which could not undertake an equally radical program,

14 https://ash.harvard.edu/publications/understanding-ccp-
    resilience-surveying-chinese-public-opinion-through-time

have been hamstrung by archaic agrarian structures ever since). This brings us to a crucial point in understanding the way the Communist party deals with its opposition, cornering it into taking up unpopular positions that lose the support of the masses. The most recent example would be when its intense psychological repression of the pro-democracy movement in Hong Kong drove its proponents into an alliance with the highly unpopular regime of Donald Trump.

China has embarked on substantial reforms since the late 1970s, under the leadership of Deng Xiaoping. The economic opening up continued under the successive leadership of Jiang Zemin, Hu Jintao and now Xi Jinping. The western world had expected a dramatic collapse of the Communist Party in China *à la* the USSR. Indeed, the 1989 pro-democracy protests were heralded as the breaking point for the Chinese regime but instead were crushed with great brutality. The reason that the party has been able to maintain its vice-like grip over the people is that it has a diffuse network of party workers, whose inputs are used to decode the aspirations of the Chinese people. Many commentators have pointed this out that the party has an implicit pact with the Chinese people that the people will enjoy a higher quality of life than ever before, if they do not seek to destabilize the regime. The rapid economic transformation of China has been the result of this pact.

The main purpose of the state-guided process of economic growth, which is termed as 'market socialism', has been to solidify the support for the state by distributing the effects of rapid economic growth among the largest sectors of the populace. These actions are not taken with any particular altruistic reasons in mind. Let us bear in mind that China has lifted nearly 850 million people out of absolute poverty since the 1990s[15]. It hopes that these developments will help it escape criticism on human rights records, and that the people who have benefitted from such policies will act as a bulwark against any destabilizing force to the regime.

User Data and Social Credits

Artificial Intelligence and the collection of user data have had an intimate link, and the collection and organization of this data is probably the field in which AI has advanced the most. The rise and growth of social media has made the collection and organization of user data possible at an industrial scale[16]. Before we move on to the question of Social Credits, we must look into the way credits work normally all over the world.

Most of us are acquainted with credit points that are provided by credit card companies, e-commerce sites, and chain stores among others. The purpose had been initially to provide incentives to customers in order to retain their loyalty. Moreover, it could help stores inform customers about their products based on their preferences as suggested by their transaction histories.

---

15   https://www.worldbank.org/en/country/china/overview

16   https://data.london.gov.uk/blog/how-user-data-is-becoming-the-ultimate-marketing-commodity/

The other kinds of credits we may concern ourselves with are credit ratings that are provided by rating agencies[17]. The vulnerabilities of credit rating agencies have demonstrated to what extent these credits can influence our lives[18]. Particularly, we shall concern ourselves with credit ratings for individuals, which often limit our ability to borrow money for any particular purpose. AI has seen massive use in the development of credit scores across the world, with neural network ensembles being used to predict bankruptcy[19]. The H20 AI points out the distinction between traditional credit scoring methods and AI-based credit scores[20]. One of the uses of AI is to root out 'churners', who have a large number of reward credit cards but are not profitable to their issuers. On the other hand, the ability of AI to provide a more granular analysis of credit history than the older scorecard system means that more people, who might have been unfairly denied credit in the previous system have a better shot.

AI has also allowed for this diverse set of data to be cross-referenced in a manner that helps unravel the deeper relationships that underpin our consumption patterns. As discussed above, the proliferation of social media platforms has allowed for the collection of user data to occur on an industrialized scale. We have previously commented

17   https://www.investopedia.com/terms/c/creditrating.asp
18   https://www.csoonline.com/article/3444488/equifax-data-breach-faq-what-happened-who-was-affected-what-was-the-impact.html
19   https://www.sciencedirect.com/science/article/abs/pii/S0957417407001558
20   https://www.h2o.ai/solutions/usecases/credit-risk-scoring/

upon the role played by recommender systems in social media, and it has become crucial to understand how such AI-driven change has drastically transformed the market for user data. Most social media platforms harvest user data in order to provide their clientele with a readymade and interactive demographic database. The potential for transforming the structure of the market itself becomes increasingly clear as these three distinct systems become integrated. This is especially true in developing parts of the world where a growing middle class is emerging, with very little access to credit. The potentiality for the use of social media in credit scoring has been noted by researchers from Wharton[21]. Thus, one's online existence is likely to determine the access to credit that a person may possess.

Social Media has also provided a platform for those who earn through content creation, an avenue that our mainstream financial institutions are yet to recognize. In the United States alone, content creators earned an estimated $6.8bn, mostly in terms of ad revenue. Karat, a start-up that offers financial services to content creators, has launched the Karat Black Card, which offers credit lines starting at $50,000 to content creators[22]. Here, creditworthiness is reliant on multiple factors including user engagement, diversification of revenue streams, and even how often they respond to emails. Given the

21 https://knowledge.wharton.upenn.edu/article/using-social-media-for-credit-scoring/
22 https://www.wired.com/story/karat-influencer-credit-card-social-media-stats/

expansion of the gig economy and with more people turning to online sources of income in order to supplement their earnings, it is clear that our credit ratings will have to take into account a vast array of factors. And if recent trends are any indicator, then AI will find an increasingly indispensable role in our access to credit, even in the parts of the world where a single authoritarian party doesn't reign supreme.

The Purpose of Social Credits in China

The social credit model of China plays into the purpose of gauging the mood of the Chinese people and what they demand, which as we are aware is crucial to the iron-grip of the Communist Party of China. In developing an all-encompassing system, the party is able to regulate the market in accordance with the way it sees resonant with its own need for stability. In his book *Discipline and Punish*, the French philosopher, Michel Foucault describes the manner in which the state's coercive machinery is steadily replaced by a system of 'social surveillance', which is manifested through the metaphorical 'panopticon'[23]. While Foucault had imagined this as a diffuse system that is a byproduct of several social processes, the Chinese state actively seeks to develop such a diffuse mode of surveillance as a matter of policy.

The possibility of integration of various online platforms with credit ratings agencies has already

---

23   Aside from *Discipline and Punish: The Birth of the Prison*, Foucault develops these themes in *The Archaeology of Knowledge* and *The Birth of the Clinic*.

been noted, which has given the Chinese government a readymade formula for the purpose of extensive surveillance that it intends to perform. The Chinese government has highlighted the necessity to bolster its domestic consumption with its 'Dual Circulation' theory[24]. This is only possible if Chinese citizens behave as 'proper' and 'responsible' consumers as desired by the Chinese Communist Party. By incentivizing a particular mode of consumptive and online behaviour, there is an attempt to reshape the market. We have discussed elsewhere that even the basic concept of labour itself is being defined more through the process of consumption than the process of production with the emergence of a 'digital capitalism'. It is in this process that the Chinese government feels the need to intervene as it is aware of the narrative of economic growth that keeps it in power.

In developing the social credit system, essentially the Chinese government is attempting to utilize AI in supplementing the task of developing 'trust'. In modifying the code of conduct that Chinese people engage in, the party hopes to transform the market itself, shaping consumer behaviour in a manner it deems 'legitimate' and 'proper'[25]. The party has so far relied on its network of members and activists to engage with the

24 https://www.scmp.com/economy/china-economy/article/3110184/what-chinas-dual-circulation-economic-strategy-and-why-it

25 The manner in which the ideas of production and consumption are shaped by AI have been discussed in the chapter titled *AI and Work Culture*.

common people of China, but now it feels that the use of AI alongside this pre-existing network provides it with greater security. The great Chinese firewall has ensured that the greater part of social media users in China have opted to use Chinese social media platforms, which gives the regime the kind of access to the private data of its citizens that would be unthinkable in the context of more open regimes.

Democracy or Social Credit?

This social credit model poses crucial questions not only for the future of the Chinese people's hope for the restoration of democracy but also for the institutions of democracy around the world. One major fear is that the authoritarian regimes in other parts of the world will seek to replicate these models in order to expand their own hold on power. Even in parts of the world with democratic institutions, the lack of democratic control over financial institutions will weaken the democratic foundations immeasurably. There is also a significant risk that the Chinese hold over international finance networks will allow them to use similar surveillance structures far beyond its borders. The United Front Work Department of China has been known to use its influence to coerce leaders of foreign countries to do its bidding, and the expansion of the social credit model will put even corporations and common citizens under its hold[26].

---

26 https://www.tandfonline.com/doi/full/10.1080/24761028.2019.1 627714

It is imperative to adjust democratic structures so that democracy can not only survive but rather thrive within the changing paradigms of credit flow. This means handing greater control of user data on social media platforms to the users themselves. Bringing all online platforms within the ambit of democratically controlled institutions can be the first step towards this process. All online platforms need to be incentivized to maintain the highest level of transparency towards their users, enabling users to take up informed decisions regarding what aspects of their lives may be open to financial institutions. Perhaps most importantly, it is imperative that an honest, open dialogue be held globally and locally regarding the changing nature of credit networks.

04. INDUSTRY AUTOMATION AND THE RUST BELT IN THE US

"There is a cult of ignorance in the United States, and there has always been. The strain of anti-intellectualism has been a constant thread winding its way through our political and cultural life, nurtured by the false notion that democracy means that 'my ignorance is just as good as your knowledge'."

– Issac Asimov

When Donald Trump announced his candidacy in 2015, most people didn't take his candidacy seriously[27]. After all, he was considered a brash, eccentric billionaire with a penchant for appearing on reality TV. He was not 'presidential' by any stretch of the American imagination and was largely dismissed in mainstream media as a 'joke' candidate. Yet, as the Republican primary went on, Trump displaced several mainstream and established Republicans to clinch the nomination. He was met in the presidential election by democratic candidate Hillary Clinton, who had decades of experience in the administration, including her most recent stint as

---

27 https://newrepublic.com/article/123228/how-donald-trump-evolved-joke-almost-serious-candidate

Secretary of State in the Obama administration. It is worth mentioning here that Hillary too met significant challenges from the openly socialist Bernie Sanders (whose candidacy was also written off initially as a weak challenge at best). Throughout 2016, most poll predictions showed that Hillary would get a comfortable victory. She clearly was the more 'acceptable' candidate on paper, and Trump was increasingly seen as a 'fringe' candidate, who was unabashed about his racism, misogyny and overall repulsiveness. How did Trump manage to clinch victory, despite losing the popular vote?

The Rust Belt and the 'Flyover Country'

The end of the Second World War saw a massive expansion of the welfare state in the US, allowing for one of the most prosperous eras in US history. This period also saw the start of the decline of manufacturing in the US. The North-Eastern region and the Great Lakes region in the US had been developed as a major home for manufacturing since the early 1800s up until the end of World War II. When manufacturing jobs slowly began to shift to Europe and Asia, these regions started to decline slowly. Later, as Asian economies started developing a robust manufacturing sector, more and more manufacturing jobs were lost. The rise of manufacturing in China and more recently in places like Vietnam has resulted in absolute economic devastation in these economies. Similarly, trade deals like NAFTA dealt a death blow to a number of jobs like auto-manufacturing into neighbouring countries of the US like Mexico and Canada[28]. The region that once been at the heart of manufacturing, was now called the 'rust belt' in reference to the abandoned factories and factory-towns that lie littered across the landscape.

This is only one side of the story. The other, even more crucial, aspect of the story is the role played by automation. It has been estimated that nearly 7 million jobs were lost to automation between 2004 and 2009 in the US, with most of the job losses among workers without a college degree[29]. While there has been some growth in GDP in the US, as a result of the trade deals, most of this growth has been concentrated in the financial and tech sectors, concentrated along the eastern and western coastal regions of the US. This has resulted in large parts of the central US, which have been left out of this narrative of development, being referred to as a 'flyover country'. Many Americans have come to resent what they view as the arrogance of the 'coastal elites', and have developed a deep distaste for their culture and politics.

This deep resentment manifested in myriad ways, especially through the wholesale rejection of traditionally progressive politics. The 'Culture Wars' which we mentioned previously emanate from this deep-seated resentment of one part of the US populace for the

---

28   https://knowledge.wharton.upenn.edu/article/naftas-impact-u-s-economy-facts/

29   https://www.forbes.com/sites/amysterling/2019/06/15/automated-future/?sh=5183c97f779d

other part. Very often debates, which are trivial, like transgendered people's access to toilets, availability of cheaper healthcare options, the huge burden of student loans on millions of young Americans or control over the use of firearms, generate acrimonious tensions and are amplified by corporate media houses[30].

Automation and US Politics

We have seen previously how automation exacerbated the process of job loss in the US, which had wide-ranging social consequences. Thus, while in places like Silicon Valley in California, which has benefitted enormously from the process of automation, the increasing capabilities of AI are seen as an unadulterated positive, others have become increasingly sceptical of modernity itself. The deep distaste for 'elite' culture and politics in the US has resulted in Trump's brand of right-wing populism. Thus, while a cosmopolitan culture is admired in coastal cities as bringing talented individuals to the United States, in Middle America, it is conflated with the increasing loss of jobs with immigrants being prioritised ahead of people from the country. Thus, when Trump calls for restrictions on immigration, one part of the US cheers while the other part looks horrified. As newer environmental regulations are sought by coastal cities, which feel threatened by the

---

30 In the chapter titled *The Cambridge Analytica Kerfuffle* we have analysed the way in which media and social media play a role in the creation of 'Culture Wars'. However, it must be born in mind that there are deep-rooted problems that form a material basis for the conflict.

effects of climate change, more rural and inland parts see a conspiracy to further hamper economic activity.

While automation has transformed America once, the growth of AI seems poised to do it again, and the developed coastal parts may not be immune to its effects. Countries like China have sought to position themselves as the frontrunners of the AI game, with growing investments in tech like 5G, which can accelerate the overall role of AI in their society. The region around the Pearl River delta is being developed by Beijing as the new 'Silicon Valley'. Automation has faced major hurdles in the trucking industry, where many truckers fear that they will be replaced by automated vehicles in the near future[31]. Automation of cabs could potentially lead to millions losing their jobs[32]. It is increasingly possible that unless newer jobs are created in sectors that can operate with similar levels of skill and comparable or higher wages, there will be stronger resistance to these processes in the US.

US politicians have largely been unwilling, if they are even capable, to address these problems. The skyrocketing cost of education and the snail-paced growth in income mean that fewer Americans are financially equipped to gain the kind of skills that would make them relevant to the increasingly tech-centred economy. Attempts to shift workers from carbon-heavy industries like mining

---

31   https://www.theguardian.com/technology/2017/oct/10/american-trucker-automation-jobs

32   https://globalnews.ca/news/4550641/self-driving-automated-cars-jobs-killed/

and oil have invited a terrible backlash to the recently elected Biden administration[33]. This is largely because the burden of 'transitioning' to a new industry with uncertain prospects has been put on the workers themselves. The use of innocuous words like 'transitioning' does not take into account the kind of emotional stress that such processes create. Firstly, the training provided is rarely free and almost never provides for a basic income during the transitional period. Secondly, there is no guarantee of jobs being available in the sectors for which training is provided, as the market in itself is a constantly transitioning one. Thirdly, given that most fossil fuel jobs were usually well paying with union-negotiated benefits, which most 'green' sectors lack, most workers would continue to suffer from economic insecurity. Combining these factors with the fact that transitioning from one employment to another after decades of employment in a particular industry is an emotional toil that requires delicate handling. One doesn't after all ask business executives to work as farmhands during times of economic downturn.

Most establishment American politicians seem to be incapable of handling the changes brought about by the ongoing trend of automation. AI possesses the capability to fundamentally transform both the workplace and our conceptualisation of work[34]. The US administration, on

---

33 https://www.bloombergquint.com/technology/miners-and-oil-workers-hear-insults-in-biden-talk-of-better-jobs

34 A detailed discussion on the changing nature of work is discussed in the chapter titled

the other hand, believes that simply providing industries with tax incentives and business 'friendly' policies will help keep 'American' jobs. This is a fundamental misunderstanding of where the 'jobs' are going since it is premised on the idea that the economy is a stagnant phenomenon with a limited number of employment opportunities that are geographically distributed.

Is Another World Possible?

US culture had responded to the questions posed by automation in the 1980s and 90s, with films like *The Terminator* series and *The Matrix* trilogy, focusing on an apocalyptic conflict between humans and machines. We have let go of some of these fears as technology has made its way into our lives and smartphones and devices have made their way into our lives. This peace cannot be taken for granted as AI increasingly penetrates our lives and livelihoods. The problem lies with the fact that most of us had thought of technology as a 'neutral' arbiter of the problems we face collectively as humanity. Tech cannot solve problems that we as a collective society refuse to confront; however, certain tech billionaires may champion battery-powered cars and colonies on Mars as the panacea to all of humanity's ills.

A zero-sum approach to a dynamic economy is one of the most regressive ways to approach the economic question, but it is increasingly finding more takers, which can only result in further economic stagnation and a technological rut. Unfortunately, here in India as well similar templates of undoing social welfare programs have been promoted as a solution to the ills of economic slowdown as a means of drawing in foreign investment by using India's 'demographic dividend'. While China, with a comparable population to that of India, is looking forward to boosting domestic consumption, our focus has been on increasing the size of the 'gig economy' and 'at will employment', both of which increase the volatility of the consumer market[35]. This isn't to say that the Indian economy shouldn't be opening up, but hedging our bets on a manufacturing model that is increasingly made irrelevant by the growing complexity of AI is a clear recipe for disaster.

The solution isn't as remote as some may be led to believe. The problem lies with the fact that a lot of the work traditionally done by humans are being taken over by AI, which has left many people with precarious existences. This is bad news for the economy as well, since the market for consumer goods plummets with shrinking disposable incomes. We had dealt with similar problems during the Great Depression by developing robust government programs. The young US Congresswoman, Alexandria Ocasio-Cortez, along with the long-time Senator, Bernie Sanders, has proposed a similar program, termed *The Green New Deal*, which improves the overall condition of working people in the US. Similarly, the proposals

---

35   In the chapter *China's Social Credit Model,* we have outlined the Chinese government's bid to boost internal consumption through its social credit model.

for lowering (or even abolishing) tuition fees in colleges, will be helpful in gaining useful skills to cope with the changing job markets. Universal Basic Income (UBI), if implemented with proper safeguards, can not only boost consumer demand but even ensure that the vast majority of people do not have to settle for the job with the lowest possible risk, even improving entrepreneurial risk-taking ventures, which is likely to drive innovation.

Not only is another world possible, but we are also stepping into that new world on a daily basis, and it is upon us to prepare ourselves for the challenges that face us. There is unlikely to be an apocalyptic takeover of Earth by sentient machines; however, an apocalypse may well come to us in the form of a world that is increasingly divided between 'haves' and 'have-nots'. Current economic trends have us competing with technology by increasingly exploitative conditions at work and little pay. This is a fundamentally unsustainable model. Those who will continue to follow it are doomed to become rust belts of the world. AI technology promises to free up humans from the drudgery of everyday labour; let's not subject the vast section of human society to the same once again. Our social organisation must transform itself to be suited to these new conditions.

05. ARTIFICIAL INTELLIGENCE AND THE QUESTION OF RACIAL JUSTICE

"If you torture data long enough, it will confess to anything."

– Ronald H Coase

We had assumed for a long time that discriminatory attitudes like racism, sexism and xenophobia would come to an end as technology would bind human society into a tightly knit and interlinked community. As we have seen through the pages of the previous chapters, technology is incapable of solving a problem without us acknowledging such discrimination in the first place. When Microsoft launched *Tay*, an AI chatbot on Twitter, it soon started spurting racist language, which it had picked up from users[36]. This leads to the question that, how do other human behaviours influenced by our embedded racial consciousness influence the development of artificial intelligence?

What is Race and Racism?

In order to understand how AI is influenced by racism, we must seek to understand how racism emerged in our

---

36   https://www.theverge.com/2016/3/24/11297050/tay-microsoft-chatbot-racist

contemporary world in the first place. As with many other issues, we need to look into our own past in order to understand the origins of racism. Most of our ancestors, be it the Ancient Greeks, Romans, Egyptians, Indians or Chinese, were aware of the physiological differences among people in various geographical parts of the world. Yet they never considered race, as we understand it, as a very useful social marker. This is not to say discrimination did not exist, as it clearly did with the various forms of social hierarchy that we read throughout history. Biologists have pointed out that Race itself is an ambiguous biological category, at best.

Race started featuring prominently in the consciousness of Europeans as the 'Age of Exploration' brought them into sustained contact with various cultures of the world. The conquest of the Americas and the mass enslavement and domination of the people of these lands brought these questions to the forefront of their consciousness. The idea that African and Native American people were 'primitive' and 'lazy' and needed the guidance of Europeans for their redemption became a justification for this exploitation. As this exploitation became a key chain in the development of capitalism in Western Europe, the logic became commonly accepted throughout the 'White' European parts of the world. It is through the forced labour of African slaves that modern industries like cotton or sugarcane had a constant supply of raw materials. This racial discrimination was justified as a form of 'redemption' of African souls through labour.

Race continued to be a useful concept in the Americas even after slavery was abolished. While poor white and African-American citizens were extremely close in their economic conditions, the ideology of race maintained strict lines of difference between them, outlawing interracial interaction as much as possible. In Europe too, the 19th and early 20th century saw the emergence of 'Eugenics', i.e., a 'scientific' form of racism. This meant that 'People of Colour' from Africa, Asia and the Americas were largely removed from sharing their experience in the world of scientific and technological changes. Technology and scientific progress were considered to be nearly exclusive domains of white Europeans for their own benefit.

It has been pointed out that Race is not 'skin deep', meaning that racism emerges from a host of social, economic and even cultural factors. In the modern world where segregation and apartheid have largely been outlawed, we continue to find a phenomenon that discriminates based on one's racial identity. The disproportionate rate of incarceration of Black Americans in comparison to their white counterparts is one well-known example[37]. This disproportionate nature is visible across several issues, including access to quality education & healthcare, home ownership, and even business loans. This form of racial discrimination is called structural racism, and it isn't limited to the United States. Structural

---

37   https://www.nytimes.com/2019/06/12/us/prosecutor-race-blind-charging.html

racism can manifest in the form of discriminatory visa policies that restrict immigration from African countries, Europe and North America. Many have pointed out that the way organizations like IMF and World Bank demand 'structural reforms' against sanctioning vital loans for the development goals of impoverished African nations are themselves a manifestation of racism. The existence of racist behaviour against people from the 'Global South' has been documented in these institutions[38].

Race in AI Technology

Since the technology was largely developed in exclusion of the interests of the People of Colour, certain aspects of technological development also became exclusionary as we shall examine in a bit.

Let us take up the example of contemporary facial recognition technology and its racial aspects. One of the major concerns is the disproportionate way in which this technology may be used in order to racially profile African Americans. This is a real concern as racially discriminatory behaviour has long plagued law enforcement in the United States. Here we deal with a distinct problem that demonstrates how social biases can percolate into AI. This brings us to the history of colour photography and the subject that such photography deals with. Lorna Roth points out that such photography was mainly aimed at depicting people

38   https://atlantablackstar.com/2012/12/03/report-details-shocking-racism-at-the-world-bank/

of 'white' skin tones rather than people of darker skin tones[39]. She points out the 'skin-colour balance' was usually measured through a reference card that showed a 'Caucasian' woman (called Shirley cards). This was due to the fact that white people came to be seen as the 'default' racial category against whom all others were to be considered. While certain rectifications were made, the cultural bias towards lighter skin tones remained. The phenomenon came down to our day in the form of AI misrecognizing black faces at a higher rate than those of white people[40].

This isn't the only area in which race has become a factor in AI technology. Let us take a look at housing and access to various forms of capital. Even after slavery was outlawed in the US, various insidious forms of racism have been prevalent, both in the Southern United States, which relied on a slave-based economy, and in the North, which had opposed the practice. While segregationist policies were overt in the South, in general, such practices were not widespread in the North. Segregation came in the form of housing discrimination as well as access to schooling and other forms of capital. One practice was that of 'redlining', i.e., systematic denial of mortgages to lower-income families who were predominantly black. While the *Fair Housing Act* of 1968 outlawed this

39 https://www.cjc-online.ca/index.php/journal/article/view/2196/3069

40 https://www.wired.com/story/best-algorithms-struggle-recognize-black-faces-equally/

discrimination, its effects continue to this day[41]. In our age of Big Data, data-mining models are used to scrutinize loan applications. This has enforced discriminatory policies while remaining nominally 'neutral'[42]. Districts and residential areas, which were previously redlined, continue to be viewed with the same prism by the AI. This becomes relevant even in the case of job applications and college applications where AI is applied in the shortlisting processes.

It is impossible to talk about race in the United States without referring to law-enforcement. Many have pointed out that the police in the US have their origins in the slave patrols, who were mainly employed to nab fugitive slaves. The police have always had a racial bias; this has been pointed out in the course of several protests, which have culminated into the *Black Lives Matter* movement. The influx of AI into law enforcement has naturally failed to solve this problem. The use of AI in pre-trial bail applications has resulted in a larger number of African American under-trials being branded as in 'Risk of Recidivism', i.e., likely to commit another crime if provided bail[43]. This happened even in cases where no evidence existed for such assumptions. Predictive policing tools have been used to create 'crime weather forecast',

41 https://www.npr.org/2017/05/03/526655831/a-forgotten-history-of-how-the-u-s-government-segregated-america

42 https://www.fastcompany.com/90269688/high-tech-redlining-ai-is-quietly-upgrading-institutional-racism

43 https://www.propublica.org/article/how-we-analyzed-the-compas-recidivism-algorithm

which has led to incessant policing of African American neighbourhoods and has increased the tension between these communities and the police[44].

Examining 'Scientific' Racism

Social theorists have long sought to critique the way science has developed in the western world, where the experiences of marginalized communities and women have been neglected. The medical field has been extensively studied by social theorists as an area where medical afflictions that have affected 'Persons of Colour' have long been neglected by practitioners of medicine. This provides us with a window that allows us to have glimpses of the way in which science and race interact[45]. The problem remains that people of certain social groups are seen as 'objects of study' or as merely some sort of 'data' to be studied for the benefit of a different population group.

The existing problems of racism in healthcare are also exacerbated by an uncritical application of AI in the medical sector. Algorithms, that predict 'risk-score' for patients in order to provide critical healthcare, routinely demonstrate that black patients had more chronic problems than similarly ranked white patients had[46]. This again has to do with African Americans spending less on

---

44   https://towardsdatascience.com/anti-racism-algorithmic-bias-and-policing-a-brief-introduction-bafa0dc75ac6

45   https://www.ncbi.nlm.nih.gov/pmc/articles/PMC1120559/

46   https://medical-technology.nridigital.com/medical_technology_sep20/ai_racial_discrimination_medicine

healthcare primarily due to economic backwardness, which the algorithm interpreted as a sign of health. In a striking parallel, during the colonial era, 'natives' were often subjected to harsh conditions of labour as it was believed that their physique made them suited to conditions of work, which Europeans would not be able to tolerate.

What we can conclude from here is the 'social' nature of 'scientific' studies. Frantz Fanon has highlighted how the fields of psychiatry have been used to cover for the horrendous effect that colonialism and oppression have on the human mind by detaching psychological issues from the social contexts that give rise to them. Structural racism has long prevented psychiatrists from making serious enquiries into the role played by discrimination on the human psyche[47]. The desire of a large section of the scientific community to 'insulate' scientific studies from the larger politics of society has only served to more scientific studies in the politics of the past.

Rather than simply a collection of attitudes and racism is rooted within the socio-economic reality that shapes our global outlook. It is indeed naïve to simply assume that scientific and technological progress can be effected without examining the role played by racism in the shaping of science and technology. We had previously examined the nature of structural racism, and here it becomes extremely important to realize that the

---

47 https://www.psychiatry.org/newsroom/apa-apology-for-its-support-of-structural-racism-in-psychiatry

'structures' that we talk about are essentially institutions that we interact with in nearly a daily manner. Scientific and technological institutions are integrated into these same structures; it is more likely than not that they will be complicit in recreating these racist structures through their political and social interactions.

Can AI Solve Racism?

AI provides us with insights into the insidious manner in which structural racism works, even when the colour of a person's skin is not factored in. In our world, race has been interwoven into a host of factors in our social fabric. In countries like the United States, race can be a factor in education, access to healthcare, and social security. Therefore, when AI is employed within a certain social framework, it shouldn't be a matter of surprise that the results end up with a racial bias.

It would be misguided to brand 'science' itself as racist, and that is not our intention in this text. It is important to understand that our understanding of 'science' is not devoid of a social lens. A little more than a hundred years ago, biologists could confidently speak of 'inherent characteristics' of various races without questioning the assumptions before decades of anti-racist activism forced them to dismantle such conceptions. It is hoped that in the case of AI, similar pressures will force technocrats to look into the biases within their systems.

It is indeed possible to rectify the biases that emerge algorithmically. It is here that we see certain structural challenges emerge to such rectification[48]. Proposed solutions to rectify algorithmic bias have been struck down by the Supreme Courts in the United States since they factor-in race directly. The unwillingness to address racial discrimination head-on remains a key obstacle in the path of creating a society where technology serves all equally. The barriers are ideological and political and must thus be confronted ideologically and politically. The 'Free Market' is not the 'Great Equalizer' that we have long assumed and plays a complicit role in recreating structures of discrimination that have been a part of our history. Technology that has an umbilical relation to such economic incentives and assumptions will not be able to create a society that avails an equal opportunity to all. Tech-based solutions cannot be provided to what are essentially social problems.

---

48   https://hai.stanford.edu/blog/legal-approach-affirmative-algorithms

06. FROM WALL STREET TO WASHINGTON D.C

"When fascism comes to America, it will be wrapped in the flag and carrying a cross."

– James Waterman Wise

When far-right mobs, who have now been branded terrorists by most mainstream sources, stormed the US Capitol in January 2021, some media personalities expressed their shock. Yet anyone who had followed the growth and proliferation of the far-right in the US and the rhetoric that Donald Trump had engaged since he started his presidential campaign (it may be argued that he had been cultivating this rhetoric since he became the face of the Birther Movement, when he started questioning the fact that Barack Obama was a 'natural born' US citizen), would have no reason to be surprised. It was no surprise when the US president started questioning the legitimacy of the election results. It was no surprise that Trump would attempt to claim that votes cast against him were somehow illegal. Why would anyone be surprised when the far-right groups did exactly what they had warned that they would do?

How 'Occupy' Changed American Politics

US history has always been fractured. The genocide of Native Americans and their forcible removal from their own land, the enslavement of millions of Africans and their subsequent disenfranchisement, and the continuing discrimination against Latinx Americans, African-Americans and other minorities all have contributed to the deep animosities that have become a feature of US politics. We shall look at the divergence that had been caused by the undoing of social security, public spending and public welfare measures in the US since the 1980s, which has been collectively termed as 'Reaganomics'. Throughout the 1990s and early 2000s, mainstream public opinion in the US welcomed the reforms as an unmitigated boon. The adverse effects of the laws were felt by communities of colour in the US, which were abandoned in the story of GDP growth.

This story began to unravel with the 'Great Recession' of 2007-08. While there are nuances behind the story of the crash of the financial sector, the attempts to revive the sector through government bailouts at a time when millions of Americans were suffering from huge education loans and a housing crisis, made it evident that the 'system' itself was biased against them. Moreover, research, sponsored by the *American Civil Liberties Union* and *Social Science Research Council*, demonstrates that the crisis widened the racial wealth gap in the US[49]. This led

49   https://s3.amazonaws.com/ssrc-cdn1/crmuploads/new_
     publication_3/impact-of-the-us-housing-crisis-on-the-racial-
     wealth-gap-across-generations.pdf

to the foundational logic of the Occupy movements that started in 2011.

"We are the 99%" was the slogan of the Occupy Movement, and it caught the public's imagination like wildfire. The *Occupy Wall Street* protests started in Zuccotti Park in the Wall Street financial district in September 2011. By focusing on the 'headquarters of global finance', the Occupy protests found reverberation around the US and even the world, which was still dealing with the fallout of the 2007-08 crisis. While the protest was by no stretch of imagination 'anti-capitalist', it did introduce the vocabulary of anti-capitalism into the political mainstream of the US. In fact, none of the demands that were made by the Occupy was outside of the political mainstream in the US, which included market reforms, banking reforms, cancellation of student debts, and alleviation of the housing foreclosures among others. What made the Occupy movement distinct was its effective engagement with social media, and the overall youthful character enabled it to gain traction even as the mainstream media portrayed it as a 'socialist' movement, which was till then a taboo. The movement even pushed forward the public profile of the Senator from Vermont, Bernie Sanders, as someone who has maintained a consistent record of supporting expenditure on public welfare, healthcare and education. With the Occupy Movement smashing the taboo surrounding the word 'Socialist' in the American political vocabulary, the self-described 'Democractic-Socialist' Bernie Sanders was realistically positioned as a challenger in the Democratic Party primaries in 2016 and 2020.

While many dismissed the short-lived protests on Wall Street as a footnote in history at best, they have proven to be wrong[50]. Candidates like Bernie Sanders, who couldn't have held a candle to establishment picks like Hillary or Biden, found reasonable fighting ground, enough to become the challenger to the eventual nominee. Many of those who were with the Occupy have been crucial parts of Sanders' team or activists with the Democratic Socialists of America[51]. The Occupy protests also demonstrated the pitfalls of blind faith on social media, when after wild rumours that the rock band *Radiohead* would perform at the site of the protests, approximately hundreds of thousands of people streamed into the site of the protests[52]. Perhaps this was a sign of things to come, with fabricated stories becoming a permanent feature of contemporary social media. What Occupy could claim success was in the destruction of the neoliberal consensus that market regulations were essentially bad.

From the Tea Party to QAnon

It would perhaps be appropriate to start our enquiry with a basic review of the cultist following of *QAnon*. Essentially, the claim goes that Q, a 'high-level' official,

---

50   https://dealbook.nytimes.com/2012/09/17/occupy-wall-street-a-frenzy-that-fizzled/

51   https://www.vox.com/the-highlight/2019/4/23/18284303/occupy-wall-street-bernie-sanders-dsa-socialism

52   https://www.theguardian.com/music/2011/oct/03/radiohead-wall-street-protest

regularly drops hints about upcoming events and the inner struggle between Donald Trump and the 'Deep State'[53]. These conspiracy theorists developed a cultish following for Donald Trump, who believed the idea that his random, often incoherent rants, were actually hinting at the events that would be upcoming. This included a 'storm' which would see the mass incarceration or even execution of Marxists, socialists, Democrats and others they believed to be a part of the 'Deep State' that was thwarting Trump from achieving his aims. Over time followers of QAnon had developed a cottage industry of websites, podcasts, YouTube channels, Twitter and Facebook pages, with 'theorists' who dedicated themselves full-time pandering to the growing crowd of believers of the conspiracy theory. This has subsequently become one of the main voting bases of the contemporary Republican Party, with many supporters of the theory finding a place in the US Congress.

Before QAnon, there was the Tea Party, a grassroots movement that was primarily aimed at combatting what was perceived as the Obama administration's attempt to expand the welfare state through programs like the Affordable Care Act. The Tea Party, though preceding the Occupy protests, was essentially a repudiation of the increasingly palpable demand for state intervention into the economy and alleviated the effects of the crisis. Grasping at straws, however, the Tea Party relied on a host of conservative forces to be foot-soldiers for the

---

53   https://www.bbc.com/news/53498434

movement. While the movement lost steam by the 2012 presidential election, the platform of the Republican Party was influenced by grassroots organizing work that had been done by various Tea Party affiliates. Donald Trump infused this base with the conspiracy theory churning rhetoric that he had taken to since he became the face of the 'Birther Movement'. When he ran for office, he found a readymade base that remained essentially at his beck and call, through his vociferous use of social media to communicate with them. The Tea Party has moved conservatism into the digital era, with its network of podcasts, internet personalities, blogs and pages on social media.

We had previously discussed how recommender networks work and how the Tea Party networks swiftly gave way to the conspiracy theory peddling that we see today. Prominent figures within the Tea Party movement, like Glen Beck, were already in the business of peddling conspiracy, which helped develop an entire ecosystem based on these theories[54]. As mentioned previously, this traps users in a filter bubble of self-affirmation that negates any critical view that allows these theories to be questioned. Given the deep distrust of the government that had followed the 2007-08 economic crisis, and the lack of a reliable explanation of the reason behind the financial crisis and the apparent lack of governmental concern allowed these theories to gain ground.

54   https://doi.org/10.1016/j.osnem.2019.10 0 058

The Artificiality of Politics

In our discussion on the role played by recommender networks previously, we have demonstrated how existing political differences have been exacerbated by what has been termed the 'Filter Bubble'[55]. It would hardly be proper to lay the blame on the door of recommender networks without discussing how media houses in the US have been complicit in the process. Nearly all political formations in the US have complained of 'media bias', arguing that the media deliberately shows them in a poor light while amplifying the voices of the opposite end of the spectrum. Trump, during his presidency, repeatedly branded all criticism as 'fake news'. Media bias is indeed a phenomenon, not only in the US, but across the world, for nearly as long as politicians have had to rely on public perception in order to garner political support. The University of Michigan even outlines the biases in different media houses in its research guides[56].

Not only do algorithms determine the content that readers receive, but automated production of journalistic content means that AI determines the news that is received in newsrooms as well[57]. The viability of a news article on a particular news network and the amount of screen time a particular news story receives are also determined by the viewership that a news network has

---

55 Refer to *The Cambridge Analytica Kerfuffle*
56 https://guides.lib.umich.edu/c.php?g=637508&p=4462444
57 https://journals.sagepub.com/doi/full/10.1177/146488 4918757072

cultivated. Karen Laurie points out that news anchors have increasingly come to resemble game-show hosts[58]. This creates a feedback loop where news rather than informing people about the challenges faced by their fellow citizens becomes a part of the very fabric of the polarized discourse. The incentive for politicians is no longer to create a dialogue between the citizens but take up entrenched positions that make them cheerleaders of a particular discourse. This is why newsroom debates today no longer correspond to any constructive discussion on policy but a spectacle where pre-established talking points are repeated time and again.

Here politics becomes a part of the artificial 'spectacle' that encourages competition for the spoils of power rather than any real expression of the issues that plague the electorate. The nature of reality itself is brought into question here as social media effectively weaponizes the aesthetics of genuineness through its ability to convert interpersonal relations into an intrinsic part of the spectacle. Thus, the spectacle is able to remake both the concerns of modern politics and its consumption in its own artificial image. While people have come to recognize the presence of media bias, attempts to mitigate it cannot be successful as long as the roots of bias remain embedded. It has been pointed out in this book that the nature of the 'filter bubble' is such that even genuine searches for 'unbiased' answers will bring users to sources that confirm their views rather than ones that would

---

58   https://www.alternet.org/2002/06/news_anchor_or_games_
    show_host/146965/

enhance their ability to critically re-evaluate their own stances.

The Post-COVID Political World

There is a palpable apprehension that the crises set off by COVID-19 would result in even greater radicalization of the Trump voting base and polarization of the American political spectrum. Many media houses have reported that, with Biden being sworn in before the 'Storm', the QAnon community was in disarray, with even more radical neo-Nazi groups looking to recruit from among the supporters of the movement[59]. The COVID crisis and the subsequent economic and social hardships being set off by them means that a larger number of people might end up even more disenchanted with the liberal-democratic setup.

Evermore than before is there a need for rethinking social networks. More importantly, there is a need for an honest dialogue regarding how social networks and social media interact with our daily lives. We have advocated for broader oversight and transparency in the manner social media functions, and the development of this conspiracy theory demonstrates the incipient danger that lies in the unregulated manner in which advertising controls social media and increasingly our news media. At the same time, we need to watch out for the possibility that oversight may tend towards the development of surveillance over what is essentially a private domain.

---

59   https://www.bbc.com/news/blogs-trending-55746304

07. ARTIFICIAL INTELLIGENCE AND WORK CULTURE

"He who works with his hands is a laborer. He who works with his hands and his head is a craftsman. He who works with his hands and his head and his heart is an artist."

— Saint Francis of Assisi

We are aware of the myriad ways in which AI influences our society. One of the key distinctions between humans and animals is the way work and labour are organized. While most animals can hunt, forage and even store food, humans have complex methods of distribution of labour that enables us to organize information and preserve our technological progress over generations. Even between different human civilizations that emerged during ancient times, the methods of distribution of work and labour were fairly distinct. With the progress of modernity, most of the world has merged into somewhat of a 'supercivilization' where the laws of organization of labour are largely the same. This doesn't mean that the whole world works with the same level of efficiency or people are paid equally for the fruits of their labour. Yet one may reasonably say that the world is being integrated into a single labour market as production becomes more and more distributed. There is another tendency that has emerged as a result of the advancement of artificial intelligence. This is the displacement of creative human labour by machine labour.

A Brief History of Work and Labour

The emergence of human societies has been contingent upon the appropriation of human labour. Most trade and commerce developed as humans produced more products than they could reasonably consume. The establishment of these trade links gave rise to large, well-organized societies with a ruling class whose sole task was the organization and distribution of the task of labour. Slavery was widespread, as force was necessary in order to have production above bare sustenance levels. In ancient societies, we find slavery to be nearly a universally present institution, though at various levels and intensities. Slavery in India and Europe was different as the required amount of labour to produce beyond sustenance levels was different. We are aware of slave raids, where organized empires raided smaller and more primitive societies to capture wealth as well as slaves. The transition from slavery to feudal serfdom represented a transition in the way labour was organized. Rather than mere force, feudalism represented the hold of 'custom' and 'tradition', over the control of labour. Most serfs were born, lived and died doing the same work that their predecessors did. They worked on their farms mainly for their immediate consumption and devoted the 'surplus labour' to their feudal lords. In other places, a part of their produce was exacted as 'rent'. This arrangement could still work because labour was still a prized commodity, which was necessary.

Thus, we find that ancient societies maintained an apparatus of coercion for maintaining themselves. Under such conditions, 'unemployment' was not a viable concept as everyone already had a predestined role to serve within society. The slaves were expected to work as were the serfs with very little compensation. However, by the 16th and 17th centuries, society was being reorganized yet again. The European exploration of the Americas and Africa and the mass exploitation of both their natural resources and labour power in the form of slaves meant that certain countries now possessed more surplus products than they would ever require. This engendered a search for newer 'markets', which would absorb this surplus production profitably, which were developed in forms of colonies. As greater numbers of markets were 'opened up' through colonization, a greater incentive was present for farming processes to be modernized. We see this in the form of the 'enclosure movement' in England, which resulted in the economic ruin of thousands of serfs, who had no longer access to even their traditional land. Many were forced to crowd into cities where they had to rely on whatever work they could find and lived in the most deplorable of conditions. For the first time in human history, labour was available in surplus, which led to the emergence of unemployment. Here lies the root of what we understand as Capitalism today.

The unemployed would find work in the newly emerging factories as the 'Industrial Revolution' started, first in England and then rapidly spread into the rest of Europe. However, this employment came with no guarantees of any sort. The moment cheaper labour was available or any new technology became available, that could do away with their labour, the workers could again be returned to unemployment. Here we see the root of the conflict between workers and technological progress. The more 'efficient' technologies were available, the more workers would find themselves in a precarious condition. Europe and North America saw massive social conflict during this period as workers rioted repeatedly, destroying machines in factories. This problem also manifested in a different manner. While the power of production increased rapidly, workers could no longer purchase these products as their wages had dropped significantly. This precipitated crises that resulted in a periodic contraction of the market, mass unemployment and economic turmoil.

After the Second World War, the crisis was managed by expanding the economic rights of the workers and providing social security. The 1950s and 60s were seen as a period of prosperity in the US and Western Europe. Easy access to education, healthcare and well-paying jobs meant widespread consumption of goods and services. This period of prosperity was put to an end in the 1970s and 80s as economists started emphasizing on reducing government expenditure. Minimum wages stagnated, and the condition of workers in the west deteriorated as companies moved their production overseas where labour was cheaper due to the lingering economic influences of colonialism. Production units were further mechanized in the 1990s and 2000s, which resulted in further job losses.

If we look at the general historical trends, we find that labour is increasingly cheaper and more specialized. The way in which the distribution of labour operates is still archaic and prevents an equitable distribution of the benefits of the advancement in production. While millions face job losses, others are overworked within the same production system.

The Antagonistic Relationship between Technology and Labour

We have seen how advances in technology have resulted in increased insecurity for a large number of workers, which have helped create antagonism to improving efficiency within the workplace. Riots in early industrial societies were aimed at damaging machines in order to ensure that workers remained indispensable to the factories. A similar impulse has been noted with every significant push towards the use of mechanization for improvement in production. Most workers have very little incentive to welcome mechanization as they are seen as unwelcome intrusions in the labour market and they will reduce wages. To be fair, there is reason for the apprehension, especially given the effect of an industrial decline in various parts of the world. Most workers, who are displaced, will perennially suffer from job insecurity as their skillsets will probably have been rendered useless by technological advancements. More importantly, no effective transition programs exist that can help workers gain relevant skills with similar economic incentives.

Initially, it was mostly manual work that risked being rendered redundant by increased mechanization. Labour-intensive sectors like mining, manufacturing and agriculture saw the bulk of job losses due to mechanization in the early years. This gave rise to the idea that income is to be linked to education, with 'skilled' workers deserving higher wages as their labour is 'unique'. The growth of the IT sector has pretty much blown up this myth and demonstrated that 'skilled' work is easily replaceable by technological advancement. The proliferation of the Personal Computer in the 1980s and 90s meant that offices looked to cut the flab in their offices by laying off people employed for managing the office work. The service sector has increasingly been feeling the heat of automation as more workers are laid off in these sectors as well.

There has been a countervailing argument that the IT sector creates jobs, often well-paying ones, and these layoffs represent only a transitional process in the economy. The examples of currently non-existent jobs, like the lamp lighter or the telegraphist, are used to buff the argument up. This overlooks the fact that such transitions have social, political and economic costs, which we may or may not be willing to bear. This also stems from the presumption that production relations will remain largely stagnant even with the changing dynamics of productive labour, which is a problematic assumption to make. More importantly, we need to challenge the idea that labour and technology must always remain at loggerheads with one always displacing the other.

AI and the Appropriation of Labour

AI has accelerated the process of appropriation of labour, even in areas which were considered immune to mechanization. While the earlier wave of mechanization had largely displaced workers in labour-intensive sectors, increasingly these displacements are being visible in the tertiary sectors. The growth of AI has already made the position of workers like taxi drivers, truckers and delivery workers extremely insecure. Most of those displaced will have to eke out a living in the 'gig economy'.

On the other hand, the advancement of production has resulted in an intensification of the consumption process itself. Social theorists like Christian Fuchs have argued that the intensified process of consumption itself is manifested in the form of labour, termed as 'prosumer labour'[60]. The idea is that AI relies on constant feedback from consumers in order to be able to function sustainably. Self-driving cars, for example, have relied

60   https://journals.sagepub.com/doi/10.1177/0961463X13502117

on monitoring feedback from actual drivers, including those whom they will displace in order to develop reliable models of driving. Yet we have very little measure of this labour, let alone a sustainable model for compensation.

While AI is rightly hailed as a transformative force in the production and distribution process, the role played by consumer behaviour in shaping AI is less recognized for its economic potential. Transforming the dynamics of work isn't as far-fetched an idea as it may sound. The assembly line once transformed the nature of manufacturing and widened the ambit of available labour to the manufacturing industry. Fordism allowed for increased productivity to be matched by increased consumption, and the expansive welfare state had allowed for a period of prosperity.

Resolving the Contradiction

The key problem that lies at the heart of this contradiction is profit models that rely on 19th century production relations. Raul Ferrer-Conill introduces the concept of 'playbour' where the lines dividing the distinction between work and leisure becomes blurred[61]. David Graeber also points out that mindless drudgery of work, which seems 'useless' creates a terrible psychological burden for the worker. By 'gamifying' work, it is possible to enable workers to find meaningful engagement within their labour. Importantly, the erasure of the boundaries of the workplace that an increasingly fragmented production

61   https://link.springer.com/chapter/10.1007/978-3-319-76279-1_11

process has created is a process that is only more likely to be further exacerbated by advancement of AI. We have long been accustomed to considering technology as a supplement to human labour. Indeed, as we have seen, this has been true for the greater part of human history, where technological advancement has enabled us to be more productive while devoting an equal amount of labour-time to various productive aspects. However, as technology becomes increasingly complex, it has grown to displace the need for human labour from certain aspects of production altogether.

Dispossession cannot go on infinitely as it will ultimately result in contraction of the market. A system where technological advancement means increasing misery for the vast number of its constituents will have to either give up all hope of technological advancement or result in self-destruction. Solutions are possible once we are willing to confront the systematic inequalities engendered in our theorization of automation. Andrew Yang, who was a candidate for the Democratic Party's nomination in the 2020 presidential elections, presented the solution of a Universal Basic Income in order to supplement jobs lost due to automation[62]. While far from adequate, Yang's proposals represent a key break as a recognition of the fact that the antagonistic relationship between labour and technology must be addressed.

---

62 https://www.cnbc.com/2018/09/10/andrew-yang-universal-basic-income-to-protect-jobs-from-automation.html

08. ARTIFICIAL INTELLIGENCE IN AFRICA

"Imperialism is a system of exploitation that occurs not only in the brutal form of those who come with guns to conquer territory. Imperialism often occurs in more subtle forms, a loan, food aid, blackmail. We are fighting this system that allows a handful of men on Earth to rule all of humanity."

– Thomas Sankara

The Artificial Intelligence Revolution has been branded as the Fourth Industrial Revolution for its implication of transforming human productivity. Yet not all are positioned to equally benefit from this revolutionary potential of AI. While Europe, North America and parts of Asia seem poised to herald a new era of development, the potential seems to be limited for some parts of the world. Africa, in particular, has had a difficult relationship with 'industrial' development in Europe, which has resulted in its own destruction, subjugation and colonization. Needless to remind most readers that one of the crucial elements that made the Industrial Revolution in England possible was African slaves working in cotton plantations in North America (and Indian indentured labour as well, but that is another story). African miners continue to have to bear near-slavery conditions in order to mine minerals like Cobalt, which are crucial to the tech industry. At the same time, the rate of internet penetration remains abysmally low in the African continent which puts it at a disadvantage in the tech race. What will be Africa's role in this revolution?[63]

The Colonization of Africa

It is nearly impossible to talk about Africa without mentioning the perennially lingering presence of colonialism and neo-colonialism in the continent. Its political boundaries, economy and even culture is continuously reshaped by this lingering presence. It is perhaps prudent to deal with the issue at the outset. The colonization of Africa had started with the European 'Age of Discovery', when countries like Portugal and Spain set up factories (colonies) along the African coast, in order to act primarily as supply stops in their journeys *en route* to the Asian countries. These factories also served as points for trade with the inland, where European powers rarely ventured. Africa became a lucrative centre for trade in gold, ivory and importantly slaves, who had to work

---

63 It is important to bear in mind that Africa is indeed a large and diverse continent. Comparing countries like Egypt, South Africa and Seychelles with impoverished Sub-Saharan countries like the Democratic Republic of Congo and Angola makes little sense. However, the growing importance of Africa as a continent means that newer geopolitical ties are being forged in the continent on a dynamic basis. The African Union too plays a dynamic role that cannot really be compared with.

in plantations in the Americas. As mentioned earlier, plantation crops like sugarcane and cotton could only be sustainably produced and sent for manufacture because of the free labour provided by African slaves.

By the 1800s, most of coastal Africa was dominated by European powers and soon enough a 'Scramble for Africa' started with older European powers like Europe and France negotiating with rising powers like Germany and Italy in order to carve up the entire continent amongst themselves. After the Berlin Conference of 1885, where the division of Africa took place, most European powers sought to convert their newly acquired colonies into a profitable market and extract their resources. This resulted in brutal and horrific conditions of labour in the African continent for plantation crops, like rubber and palm oil, as well as for extraction of precious mineral resources, like diamonds[64]. In places like South Africa and Rhodesia, a brutal apartheid regime was put in place, which suppressed the political rights of native Africans. Similar occupation regimes were maintained by the French in its North African colonies like Algeria. This was done in order to ensure that Africans remained suppressed so that they could provide labour for cheap. Even as colonialism formally came to an end, the African continent found itself mired in countless conflicts which were often linked directly or indirectly to their former

---

64 Joseph Conrad's *Heart of Darkness* narrates the condition of the people in Belgian Congo. The brutal conditions of colonialism are visible in Conrad's novella.

colonizers. When we combine these histories, it becomes evident from here why Africans might be apprehensive of the possible repercussions of the AI Revolution.

Is Tech Transforming Africa?

Africa, as a growing economic powerhouse, has often been at the focus of attention with its economic potential. Many African nations have demonstrated remarkable potential for growth, with 643 innovation hubs on the continent[65]. By 2016, one-fifth of Africans had access to broadband, and this figure has doubled by now[66]. Multiple reports have pointed out that a large number of Africans have benefitted from the widespread availability of the internet, and there is an expectation that greater internet penetration will bring about greater prosperity for Africans[67]. As we have emphasized earlier, a tech revolution is rarely a 'harmless' process, especially in a continent like Africa with immense differences in access to wealth, education and other basic necessities, a 'digital divide' can have devastating consequences for parts of the population.

It may be pragmatic to start off with the more positive aspects of technological changes. Sub-Saharan Africa had always been prone to droughts, which has resulted in mass

---

65   https://interestingengineering.com/the-technology-industry-in-africa-is-growing

66   https://www.statista.com/statistics/1176654/internet-penetration-rate-africa-compared-to-global-average/

67   https://www.theguardian.com/world/2016/jul/30/africa-a-day-in-the-digital-life

famines and starvations. The use of AI-driven weather prediction technology has the potential to change that. Research has been made into the possibility of using the 'non-mystical' aspects of traditional methods of weather forecasting in fine-tuning the process of prediction[68]. Apps like *UjuziKilimo* have helped Kenyan farmers with their irrigation practices using SMS-based technology[69]. The analysis of crop diseases is another region where AI shows promise[70]. In Nigeria, the chatbot named *Kudi* has been helping users avail banking services using Facebook's Messenger app[71]. This demonstrates the potential of AI being a major component to the endemic problems that a large number of Africans seem to be facing on a daily basis.

Yet there is another aspect of tech that we seldom like to discuss, precisely because it makes us uncomfortable and complicit in violations of human rights. While Africa lags behind every other continent in terms of technological advancement, it plays a major role in the supply of Cobalt, which is a key component of Lithium batteries. The Democratic Republic of the Congo, which is the source of nearly half of the world's production

---

68   https://pubs.cs.uct.ac.za/id/eprint/831/1/p122-masinde.pdf

69   https://medium.com/@millersocent/agricultural-social-enterprise-helps-kenyan-farmers-increase-crop-yields-through-soil-analysis-65af500b64aa

70   https://www.courthousenews.com/new-ai-app-predicts-climate-change-stress-for-farmers-in-africa/

71   https://techpoint.africa/2019/03/22/it-seems-nigerian-payments-startup-kudi-has-raised-5-8m-in-a-series-a-round/

of Cobalt, has been repeatedly accused of using slaves, especially child-slaves, for the mining of Cobalt[72]. In fact, in a 2019 lawsuit by *International Rights Advocates*, nearly every major tech giant was named for their role in the illegal use of slave labour for mining Cobalt. In fact, many have pointed out that the so-called 'tech boom' in Africa is really only a new colonialist initiative emanating from Europe and North America, as the previous ones were. The *Financial Times* points out that companies like Jumia, which has been dubbed to be the 'Amazon of Africa', have hardly anything to do with Africa besides the fact that they are predominantly aimed at an African clientele[73]. Using cheap labour of impoverished Africans in order to exploit its markets while benefiting mostly European and American investors hardly seems to be a recipe for success for Africans.

The Hurdles for AI in Africa

Google's head of AI in Africa points to the significant challenges that Africans face regarding AI[74]. This includes the lack of sufficient training available on the continent which means that IT professionals often have to travel outside the country to gain the necessary skills. Often visas are denied to students of African origin, which

---

72 https://www.theguardian.com/global-development/2019/dec/16/apple-and-google-named-in-us-lawsuit-over-congolese-child-cobalt-mining-deaths

73 https://www.ft.com/content/4625d9b8-9c16-11e9-b8ce-8b459ed04726

74 https://www.bbc.com/news/business-48139212

points to a larger systematic problem of racism that plagues the development of tech. Here lies a structural hurdle to the growth of AI-based tech industries on the African continent. Another major problem that plagues the growth of AI in the continent is the low level of statistical capacity. AI relies on statistical data in order to develop its models, which makes the development of AI extremely hard in the African context.

This brings us to the problem of underdevelopment in Africa. The lack of traditional infrastructure means that as AI rapidly grows and changes the nature of jobs, Africans might find it difficult to acquire skills quickly enough to help reap the benefits. Education sectors across most of Africa already struggle with their task of providing basic facilities for STEM education, and thus the elevated requirements that are crucial in the AI centred economy might not be accessible to Africans. The lack of broadband connectivity in Africa is also a key problem that cannot simply be wished away. Approximately 267 million people in Africa do not have access to the internet, and this lack of access affects certain social groups more than others. Here lies the risk of recreating and even increasing the already existing inequalities in African societies.

The lack of availability of data, which we have mentioned earlier, has made Africa into what is called a 'Data Desert'. This is a problem that is deeply political as much as it is technological since it all boils down to the question of who 'counts' in a society. In a continent like Africa that has been fractured by the worst of colonialism, these differences often replicate colonial structures and hierarchies.

The Transformative Potential of AI

In a study conducted by the University of Pretoria, the opportunities presented by AI in key sectors are underscored[75]. Sectors like agriculture, healthcare, public services, financial services and education, can all benefit from the influx of AI as we shall see.

In Sub-Saharan Africa, 65% of the labour force works in agriculture and it contributes to 32% of the GDP. Environmental factors play a major hindrance in improving productivity in this sector. AI, along with machine learning, satellite imagery and advanced analytics, has the potential to improve productivity and efficiency at all stages of the agricultural value chain. Apps like FarmDrive, a credit-scoring platform for smallholder farmers, have been helping financial institutions reach out to creditworthy farmers within the smallholder category. AI has also helped develop 'smart farm' technologies that help document the growth of every single plant in a field, helping manage the decisions at the granular level. Similarly, the Sowing App, developed by Microsoft and ICRISAT, uses AI to study weather forecasting models in order to guide farmers to pick the ideal sowing week.

The healthcare sector is another area in which Africa has a lot of catching up to do with the rest of the world.

---

75 https://www.up.ac.za/media/shared/7/ZP_Files/ai-for-africa.zp165664.pdf

The scarcity of medical staff and medical supplies can seriously hamper access to healthcare in many cases. AI could play a major role in diagnostics, improving access to healthcare, as well as help public policy by providing greater information about the pattern of spread of diseases. One example would be that of Corti, a machine learning company from Denmark, which helps responders first make life-saving decisions by identifying any pre-existing conditions the patient may have. In other areas, bots have been used to provide a conversational interface for patients to understand more about their conditions using popular messaging apps.

The poor experience of Africans with public services can seriously erode trust with the government. Redundancy and red tape are compounded by corruption and lack of transparency. Research by the Harvard Kennedy School demonstrates that AI can play a major role in increasing the accessibility of governance by common citizens[76]. Chatbots have helped with filling out and completing documents and helped cut through bureaucratic delays. While internet connectivity across Africa has not been great, cell phones are easily accessible and services must be modified to suit these needs. Bringing government services closer to Africans will also help build trust with the government, which can go a long way to end the entrenched conflict in the region.

---

76 https://ash.harvard.edu/files/ash/files/artificial_intelligence_for_
    citizen_services.pdf

Chronic poverty has been a major problem all over Africa, and increased access to financial services is one way to mitigate the problem. The algorithmic processing of data frees up banking from the possibility of human error and reduces the risk of The Nigerian Zenith Bank Plc, providing an easy way of processing transactions, helping customers with mobile banking facilities. Another program, ALAT, operated by the Wema Bank, helps clients open up bank accounts online, also providing debit card facilities within two to three days. This easy availability of banking facilities can provide economic mobility to common Africans, which in turn can help stimulate economic growth within the region.

In a region like Africa, where traditional infrastructure can hamstring growth potential, AI can help bypass conventional bottlenecks, providing a major impetus for economic growth. While conventional technological benefits are still lacking in several parts of Africa, AI has allowed Africans to catch up with the developed world, which in turn can further fuel a process of global integration.

Towards an African Century in the AI Age

Africa has been heralded as the 'next big thing' on the technological and economic frontier as Asia had been in the 20th and early 21st centuries. Yet this optimism needs to be grounded in a sober analysis of the reality of the continent. Not all of Africa will proceed at the same pace, and these inequalities will be major challenges since they will be masked as a 'natural' outcome of the AI age. Blind pursuit of standards set by European or Asian societies might be a recipe for disaster as lucrative emulating these standards as the global benchmark for progress might seem. We have discussed elsewhere in this book how even 'advanced' societies in the western world have been facing challenges in the face of the growing role of AI in the economy. If Africa is to 'skip' the stage of traditional industrialization in order to more aggressively pursue the AI-centred growth model, it will need to proceed with extreme caution.

09. THE EUROPEAN MODEL FOR DATA PRIVACY

"They who can give up essential liberty to obtain a little temporary safety deserve neither liberty nor safety."

– Benjamin Franklin

The merger of Facebook and WhatsApp into a single entity had raised several concerns about user privacy. At the same time, it became a point of discussion that WhatsApp would maintain separate privacy policies in Europe. This brings us to an important question. What makes Europe's privacy laws distinct from the rest of the world? More importantly, what was the impetus that allowed EU lawmakers to provide for stronger privacy laws than other parts of the western world? These differences would mean that the manner in which AI could transform Europe would be significantly different from the way the rest of the world interacts with technology. An understanding of these changes could help in analysing the trajectories towards which a new Europe will move.

The European Union Explained

While the European Union is a large economy with diverse economic systems that evade broad generalisations, the presence of the common market presents a compelling argument for the treatment of the region as a distinct category. Strong social programs and the largely undiluted presence of a welfare state are a few key ways in which Europe differs from the United States, which has significant implications. In order to understand the way in which the governments in Europe and those in the rest of the world deal with issues related to the privacy of the data of their citizens, it is crucial to understand the European Union itself.

In order to understand the European Union (and its periphery), we need to understand the various overlapping agreements that are its constituents. The seeds of what we call the EU today were laid by the *Treaty of Rome* in 1957. It created the European Economic Community (EEC) signed by Belgium, France, Italy, Luxembourg, the Netherlands and West Germany. This was a successor to the European Coal and Steel Community (ECSC) that was founded in 1951 by the *Treaty of Paris*. The other important entity that must be discussed is the European Free Trade Association (EFTA) founded in 1960 by Austria, Denmark, Norway, Portugal, Sweden, Switzerland and the United Kingdom. This later evolved into what we know as the European Economic Area today. While the EFTA was developed as an alternative to the EEC and had a competitive relationship with it, cooperation soon became a necessity.

Another key area of importance is the *Schengen Agreement*, which established a common visa policy among most countries of what is known as the European Union. This is significant in a part of the world which, not a few decades ago, had been ripped apart by centuries of conflict. The Schengen Area led to the removal of internal borders between most of Western Europe. By allowing the free flow of labour within the region helped boost the economy, transforming the EU into the economic powerhouse that we know today. Finally, of course, there is the *Eurozone*, which are the countries that use the Euro as their currency. This is the most remarkable feature of the EU and one that is probably the most widely known. Integrating multiple systems of varying sizes and complexities within the framework of a single monetary is a feat that can be endlessly discussed.

Online Privacy Regulations in the European Union

The 1950 *European Convention on Human Rights* declared, "Everyone has the right to respect for his private and family life, his home and his correspondence". This has been the basis of the General Data Protection Regulation (GDPR) implemented in 2018, touted as one of the strictest globally for data privacy and security. In the chapter on *Cambridge Analytica*, we discussed the way in which the private data of users had been used (or rather misused) in order to develop algorithmic models to target users in a particular manner.

The GDPR replaced the Data Protection Directive, which originated in 1995, in order to protect the online privacy of internet users in the EU. Fundamentally, the

GDPR ensures that user consent is obtained before any data is gathered from their online activities. It also requires any data that is gathered to be anonymized in order to ensure that individual users feel secure. Importantly, it requires swift notifications of data breaches and any transfer of user data across the border to be handled in a sensitive manner[77].

One major reason that European privacy regulations are so strict is because one of its key constituents, Germany, is extremely sensitive to any breach in data privacy. There are historical reasons for this, primarily the extreme lack of privacy that many Germans endured in Nazi Germany and in East Germany during the cold war. This becomes evident as we find that things we take for granted, like Google Street View, are largely unavailable in Germany (and Austria)[78]. These historical traumas mean that Germans value privacy over 'efficiency' with a snail-paced growth in certain areas of tech such as online transactions. This shouldn't detract us from the fact that Germany has been at the forefront of tech innovation in the European Union and arguably the entire world.

The GDPR ensures that companies that operate in European cyberspace must be in compliance with its regulations. The GDPR focuses on basic identity

77 https://digitalguardian.com/blog/what-gdpr-general-data-protection-regulation-understanding-and-complying-gdpr-data-protection
78 https://bigthink.com/strange-maps/germany-street-view?rebelltitem=5#rebelltitem5

information, location, IP addresses, health information, biometric data, demographic data and political opinions that may be collected during a person's online interactions. It has been pointed out that GDPR provides extensive leeway to the regulatory authorities in describing what constitutes a 'breach' of privacy, thus closing down the possibility of companies using legal loopholes in order to collect data[79].

Can GDPR Survive?

It has often been questioned whether the GDPR can survive in a globalised world, especially as social media and digital platforms have come to dominate large parts of the world economy. While a little above 52% of marketers believe that governmental regulations like GDPR will hinder their ability to leverage user data[80], it also needs to be borne in mind that nearly 64% of people mistrust tech companies due to apprehension of misuse of data, as demonstrated by a study by Oxford Economics[81]. Thus, the odds are not stacked overwhelmingly against data privacy either, as users seek governmental regulations in order to protect their own privacy from the use by tech giants. This brings us to the

79 https://www.csoonline.com/article/3202771/general-data-protection-regulation-gdpr-requirements-deadlines-and-facts.html

80 https://www.emarketer.com/chart/226917/challenges-that-may-impede-their-ability-derive-value-their-data-driven-marketingmedia-initiatives-2019-according-us-digital-marketers-of-respondents

81 https://www.oxfordeconomics.com/recent-releases/digital-society-index-2019-human-needs-in-a-digital-world

question of how online privacy regulations can prove to be a game-changer in the world of international trade as well as for intergovernmental relations.

This has been the case with the US and EU, which have traditionally maintained close economic and geopolitical links with each other. Given that most US-based tech companies have relied on a 'service for data' model for revenue generation, it makes it exceedingly difficult for them to remain viable under such privacy regimes. There have been a number of cases against US tech companies' violation of EU privacy laws. The Google Street View Privacy Case, the Google Privacy Policy Case, the Google Spain's right to be forgotten case, as well as the case against Facebook for transferring user data from the EU to US servers, demonstrate how privacy policy concerns have been a major issue in the EU. US privacy policy measures have usually trailed those of its EU counterparts.

The fact that the US has mass surveillance protocols in place, which US-based companies are bound to follow, means that any possibility of data-sharing between the US and EU runs afoul with the GDPR regulations[82]. An attempt was made to reconcile these differences by means of Schrems II but such workarounds too failed[83]. The cause of this irreconcilability lies in the very historic nature of the origin of the diverging notions of privacy on

---

82   https://www.theverge.com/2020/7/16/21326795/eu-us-personal-data-transfer-privacy-shield-invalidated-sccs-upheld

83   https://www.brookings.edu/techstream/why-schrems-ii-requires-us-eu-agreement-on-surveillance-and-privacy/

the two sides of the Atlantic. This explains why the EU faces political pressures from its public against all possible forms of surveillance and in support of the preservation of data privacy, while the US public opinion is marked by characteristic nonchalance.

The Changing Dynamics of Tech Revenue Models

We had discussed earlier how major tech and social media companies monetize user data, which serves as the primary revenue models for these platforms. Rather than charging users for the services they provide, they mainly rely on accumulating user data on their platforms and providing targeted advertising through AI-based recommender models. Thus, growing control of users over what aspects of their private data they want out of bounds for tech companies directly affects their profit margins.

Another interesting recent case has been the ongoing tussle between the Australian government and Facebook. Simply put, the Australian government pushed for a law that mandated that tech platforms like Google and Facebook should be made to pay users at least a part of their ad revenues to media houses when their news links were shared[84]. There is an apparent logic in the proposals for two main reasons. Firstly, these platforms rely on the content provided by media houses to maintain user engagement, thus helping the platforms remain financially

---

84   https://www.vox.com/recode/22287971/australia-facebook-news-ban-google-money

viable. Secondly, the rise of social media has resulted in declining profits for traditional media as more and more users rely on social media for news. Facebook responded to these changes by blocking access to all news on the site, provoking great outrage from multiple sides. A similar case had transpired with Google as well, where Google too threatened to prevent access to Australian users. However, it seems that both platforms have managed to work out agreements with news outlets regarding revenue sharing[85].

These trends demonstrate the rapid changes that are occurring within the sector that is being shaped by various nudges, push and pull factors. Already a number of other governments in the EU and Canada are considering similar propositions as those put forward by the Australian government. It is important to note that this doesn't actually create an alternative revenue model based on preserving user privacy. Some have pointed out that this fundamentally changes very little except further enriching powerful media houses, which already have a stranglehold of news outlets. It is undeniable that the accumulation of enormous amounts of user data by online platforms has been critical to the growth of AI in our current world, but the question is how much of our privacy are we willing to sacrifice in order to retain these benefits?

We believe that at the root of this contradiction lies the tension between changing dynamics of consumption

---

85   https://www.bbc.com/news/world-australia-56107028

and production in the age of AI and the increasingly archaic model of revenue generation that both media houses and social media platforms must rely on. While it is quite easy to take up entrenched positions, either against governmental regulations or against the corporate greed of tech giants, it is important to take a look at the basic problem that plagues all these fields. It must be said that the GDPR is a commendable step towards a new internet age that can provide a more equitable path to globalisation, where one does not have to compromise with their basic human rights and dignity in order to be able to enhance their chances of success in a global market. This being said, we also need to understand why blanket governmental regulations that copy and paste the GDPR might not prove to be useful. As we saw in the case of Africa, a blind emulation of standards that have been developed in widely different contexts, might retard, rather than enhance the possibilities of development.

CONCLUSION

"The reigning economic system is a vicious circle of isolation. Its technologies are based on isolation, and they contribute to that same isolation. From automobiles to television, the goods that the spectacular system chooses to produce also serve it as weapons for constantly reinforcing the conditions that engender 'lonely crowds'."

– Guy Debord

If there is one thing that we hope readers will take away from this book, it is the desire to start a conversation on how AI is changing our world. We have repeatedly emphasized this theme precisely because getting a conversation started on the subject matter is crucial. When shocking revelations are made from the world of tech, the tendency is to blame a particular company or individual rather than an honest introspection. This isn't to say that certain companies do not place profit above their users' privacy and security, but these problems can only arise when we as users are not careful with how our data is being utilized. At the same time, we must be careful enough to understand that it is unreasonable to expect users to make 'informed' decisions when information is obfuscated behind legal jargon as well as the actual mechanisms through which the algorithmic manipulation of our choices takes place.

What we have discovered through these chapters is that AI doesn't create problems as much as it makes existing problems visible. Suppressing the visibility of the problems doesn't necessarily entail the suppression of these problems altogether. Let us take the example of Cambridge Analytica. CA didn't develop Facebook or invent targeted marketing strategies. What it did was use the available technology (though in an unethical manner) and use it to develop campaigns in a manner that essentially polarized voters rather than inform them. While the methods are indeed controversial, advertisers have been using similar strategies for years without stoking 'controversy'. Another example would be the effect of redlining in AI, and its resultant lack of access to social capital for black Americans. Here too, the problems have been present in an implicit manner and have been raised by activists for decades. When AI came into the mix, the extent of the problem became explicit and we no longer had an excuse to evade the questions that they raised.

The more entrenched problem is that we have sought to tackle these issues with archaic institutions and archaic approaches to problem-solving. The US addressed the problem of segregation by outlawing visible forms of explicit segregation but failed to look at the deeper socio-economic roots of the problem or address them in any meaningful manner. The result was that subsequent US administrations brushed these issues under the carpet where they continued to simmer. In the case of China, we placed the issue of social surveillance under a lens of human rights and led ourselves to believe that widespread international outrage would be enough to reverse the process. Such an approach remained blind to the real motivations of the Chinese state in expanding its control of the market, especially in the age of AI. In fact, we have rarely discussed how transformative the effect of AI will be on the labour market, especially in changing the existing relationship between capital, consumption and labour. In this book, we have sought to get the ball rolling on these discussions.

In fact, our understanding is that consumption, rather than labour, will become the primary drivers of economic change as AI will replace both skilled and unskilled workers in several sectors. Transitioning from a labour-centric to a consumer-centric economy will prove to be a challenge, especially in the Global South where governments are still focused on freeing up labour from 'unproductive' areas and engaging them in more 'productive' industries. While there are several factors that will affect this dynamism, and making predictions under such circumstances are futile, if the developing world cannot ramp up consumption within its own market, the AI-centric economic system might simply become a repeat of the form of colonialism that we had seen between the 17th and 20th centuries. Indeed, this is the fear that many Africans express, not without reason, given that large parts of the continent risk being left behind in this dynamic world.

Attempts to address these problems through simple policy measures have run into their own problems as we see them in the case of the European Union. Given that many digital platforms monetize by enabling advertisers to access user data, this leaves parts of the world where users are less able to pay to access online services at a significant disadvantage. We also saw how widely varying historical concepts have led to the various approaches to the algorithmic appropriation of data that occurs all around the world. While a large number of Europeans are supportive of the state's intervention in the economy, a significant number of Americans would consider such attempts at developing a welfare state against the very fabric of the US. On the other hand, while Americans are largely unconcerned by the extensive surveillance mechanism that their government operates, any compromise with the security of personal data in the EU is unacceptable. This creates significant problems given our contemporary Westphalian system of sovereignty, as data is increasingly developing a transnational characteristic.

Broadly speaking, all these problems can be categorized as issues that are generated when archaic socio-economic structures are confronted by newer forms of technological reality. This brings us to the question, what are the appropriate responses to such changes? To answer this, we need to recognize that our contemporary form of neoliberal capitalism and capitalism itself is in a process of historical change. The structures that we take for granted like law courts, nation-states and a framework for international trade have all been developed through and during the process of the development of capitalism. It led to concepts like representative democracy, rule of law and recognition of private property. These are the frameworks within which we seek to operate but also are the ones that are likely to be transcended by newer methods of production. Seen in this manner, we shall be able to understand our current conundrum in the right context. It must also be kept in mind that the same forms of transition aren't happening uniformly across the world.

Let us bear in mind the last major transformation that the world experienced as Feudalism went into decline and Capitalism unleashed newer productive forces on the face of the planet. Europe, which was at the epicentre of these developments, was able to dominate the global discourse for centuries, and we are still feeling their effects. Rather than the divine rights of the kings, we found a new source of sovereignty in the will of the people. Colonialism was driven by the need for newer markets for finished commodities, as well as a source of raw material for cheap. The productivity of human labour went through the roof as we discovered machines capable of multiplying the productivity of a worker by tens or even hundreds of times. It would therefore not be unreasonable to expect similar transformative forces to be unleashed onto society by these developments in the world of tech. We have already seen that AI has fundamentally reorganized our production processes far beyond what could be imagined in the last century, which has resulted in consumption being the primary driver of the new economic processes.

Missed Opportunities

There are certain aspects we have not been able to discuss in detail here and which we hope to address in future works. While we have discussed the varied role played by AI in transnational contexts and specifically the impact of AI on data sharing between the US and the EU, we have been unable to discuss the role of AI on international relationships specifically. AI has an ever-growing role in the world of finance and international trade. Many governments have started relying on AI to guide them through the process of international diplomacy[86]. Moreover, the rise and growth of social media have contributed to the consolidation of political forces in an unprecedented manner, which in turn has allowed both democratic and anti-democratic forces to take advantage. Perhaps the most spectacular expression of these changes has been with the Arab spring that started in 2010-11, mainly fuelled by people using social media platforms to subvert the traditional modes of control that dictators in the Middle East and North Africa exercised.

These discussions also bring us to the use of AI in counter-terrorism operations, as well as the use of social media by terrorism networks to get new recruits.

---

86 https://www.diplomacy.edu/blog/event-summary-impact-ai-diplomacy-and-international-relations

Surveillance, as we have seen, has evoked various responses from members of the public. One reason why people are willing to tolerate surveillance is the detection and elimination of the threat of terrorism. The idea is that by providing AI with the ability to algorithmically mine through the data of hundreds of millions of users, we will be able to detect the possibility of an act of terrorism before it is committed. This is problematic, not only because it would be an absolute subversion of our existing conceptions of justice but also because of the fact that as we saw with racism, the fact that we target certain ethnic groups for committing acts of terrorism far more than others. A similar case can be made against the use of AI in enforcing criminal justice and in the maintenance of law and order.

We would have also liked to include a discussion on the role played by AI in helping understand phenomena like climate change, especially with the possibility of hundreds of millions of people facing dislocation worldwide. A detailed discussion on the effects of climate change would have helped. The recent massive power outage in Texas points to the danger posed by erratic weather patterns that climate change is likely to affect not simply coastal regions but also regions inland and in unprecedented manners. There is also an ever-increasing danger of massive crop failures globally as climate patterns change throughout the world. AI can both help prepare for the incoming danger posed by climate change as well as help us resist the process to as great an extent as possible.

Another region where AI could prove to have a transformative effect is that of education. Online educational portals have flourished, but the effect is nowhere near what the potential suggests. There has been a plethora of criticism of the incoming digital divide between students who are able to avail education online, and those who aren't, which must be addressed if we are to move forward in this direction. Since teaching itself is a community activity, it is somewhat difficult to automate, and attempts at automation have been exemplary failures. However, AI can be used to help both students and teachers to identify lapses in pedagogical exercises and replace our current system of learning by memorization.

To Sum Up

As AI itself is an ever-evolving field, it makes any prediction on its posited direction very difficult, and that is clearly not our objective here. What we want to analyse here is the existing reach and potential for the growth of AI in terms of its socio-economic dynamics. Without venturing into a jargonized technicality, we hope to ensure that readers find a fundamental grasp of the shifting terrains of AI application in various fields. Interdisciplinarity has already become a catchword in various academic settings that allows for the transgression of convention boundaries of knowledge, which is a key breakthrough in this regard. These knowledge-flows must go beyond academic settings into the industry.

One of the key takeaways, as we discussed previously, is that our social, economic and political institutions are being challenged by AI in a transformative manner. This transformation must effectively transform all these institutions, either by rendering them hollow or overhauling them in its own way. As we have seen through the chapters, it has had a transformative effect on political campaigns and agendas, governance and administration, labour, consumption, race relations and community building, geopolitics, healthcare and education. The fact that our institutions have been unable to respond to these drastic and undeniably rapid changes means that conscious effort must be made in these directions that go beyond cosmetic policy proposals. This does not mean that we must not propose policy changes. Quite to the contrary, suggestions for policy changes must become more vigorous as must debates that are held surrounding such changes. What must be taken into account is that such changes will affect all cross-sections of society in an uneven manner. In fact, the way we propose hypothetical policy changes in a top-to-bottom format must be replaced by a ground-up that takes into account the horizontal forms of dialogue and debate. We hope that through this book we will be able to respond adequately to these challenges.

THE BOOK IN A NUTSHELL

1. The book explores the role of artificial intelligence and its application in contemporary society.

2. It explores how AI interacts with contemporary societal structures in order to transform their essence.

3. Existing social problems too are sometimes thus replicated and amplified by the role of AI.

4. This is because of how deeply AI development is tied to contemporary economic structures.

5. Technocratic solutions cannot offer reprieve from social problems.

6. In many cases the emergence of algorithmic inequality demonstrates deep-rooted and unseen forms of inequality.

7. The solution is to rely less on technocratic expertise and incorporate more social scientific criticism.

MAY I ASK YOU FOR A SMALL FAVOUR?

We are pleased to announce our latest publication titled "*The World as a Neural Network*", where we grapple with the critical question of the impact of Artificial Intelligence on our society as a whole. We explore a host of issues ranging from racism to global geopolitics within the pages of our book and hope to give our readers a holistic picture of how the world around us is changing.

We hope you will take a look at our work and find time to provide us with your review.

BOOKS BY THE AUTHORS

The first book published by the authors was on January 14th, 2021, on women empowerment.

The book is titled "Empower to Transform".

Description of the book

"Empower to Transform" is an in-depth analysis of gender inequality and some of the concepts that revolve around it. This aspect that has received a lot of attention from researchers still remains a mystery to most people. Due to the lack of understanding on the matter, most women find themselves unable to pull through from the chains that oppress and prevent them from achieving success.

This analysis starts by exploring the effects and dangers of atrocities on women. It then digs deeper to matters related to equality at home and work, diversity and inclusion, women in leadership, role of men in women empowerment and empower to transform.

Other than introducing the society to the merits of women empowerment, this is a guide that will motivate and inspire women of all ages, races and ethnicities to revolt against the social injustice that they face.

It's not your ordinary self-help book as it dives into the core issues that need to be addressed when it comes to empowering women. That aside, this book also touches on some of the most sensitive topics such as diversity and inclusion which not only affect women but also people of different races.

Full of well-researched and discussed topics, this is a book that will change your perspective towards gender equality. Written for both women and men, "Empower to Transform" leaves you with a lot of valuable information long after you have turned the final page.

REACH OUT TO THE AUTHORS

Website:

Authornirajabandi.com

Email: contact@authornirajabandi.com;

Social media handles:

Instagram: bandiniraja

https://www.instagram.com/bandiniraja/

Facebook page:

Niraja Bandi

https://www.facebook.com/niraja.bandi.1